WILLIAM WORDSWORTH

William Wordsworth at the age of 28.

WILLIAM WORDSWORTH

The Wandering Poet

by

Natalie S. Bober

THOMAS NELSON INC., PUBLISHERS

Nashville   New York

Copyright © 1975 by Natalie S. Bober

All rights reserved under International and Pan-American Conventions. Published in Nashville, Tennessee, by Thomas Nelson Inc., and simultaneously in Don Mills, Ontario, by Thomas Nelson & Sons (Canada) Limited. Manufactured in the United States of America.

First edition

Library of Congress Cataloging in Publication Data

Bober, Natalie S.
  William Wordsworth, the wandering poet.

  Bibliography: p.
  SUMMARY: A biography of the English romantic poet whose relationship with Samuel Taylor Coleridge was a source of great inspiration to him.

    1. Wordsworth, William, 1770–1850—Biography—Juvenile literature. [1. Wordsworth, William, 1770–1850. 2. Poets, English] I. Title.
PR5881.B6   821'.7 [B] [92]   74–32392
ISBN 0-8407-6431-6

In loving memory of
my father,
who early taught me
the joy of reading

Contents

Acknowledgments

I am deeply grateful to my three children—Marc, for his criticism and encouragement during the early stages of my work, Steve, my own present-day Wordsworth, and Betsy, for sharing her mother with a typewriter—and to my mother, who painstakingly proofread and indexed the book.

I owe a great debt of gratitude to Phyllis Deuel and Phyllis Coniglio, who typed the entire manuscript, and to L. J. Davis, whose advice and suggestions headed me in the right direction.

Perhaps the greatest thanks are due my young friend Lisa Toffler, who carefully read the manuscript chapter by chapter and offered thoughtful and incisive suggestions, and whose honesty and enthusiasm encouraged me to keep writing.

And to my husband—for taking me to England and to the Lake District, the original inspiration for this book, for patiently and happily visiting Hawkshead, Dove Cottage, and all the surrounding area in which Wordsworth lived and grew, for his beautiful photographs of the area, and for his faith in me—my love and appreciation.

WILLIAM WORDSWORTH

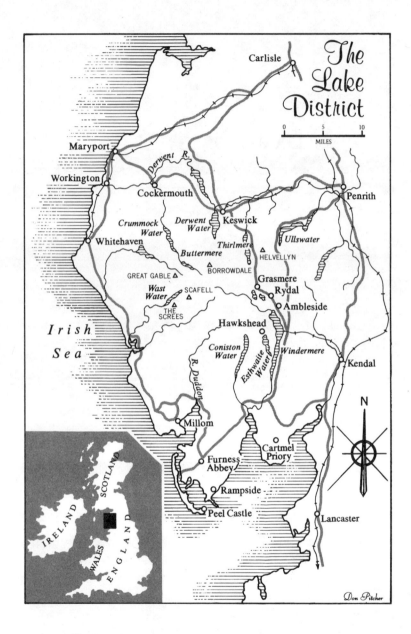

Chapter 1

Oh! Pleasant, Pleasant Were the Days

The little boy bounded up the stairs of his grandfather's house in Penrith, in northern England, and ran down the hall. He was stopped by the nurse, who cautioned him to be quiet, because his mother was resting. As he peeked into the room, he saw his mother, young and beautiful, but ominously still and pale, lying in the large four-poster bed. His father was standing in front of the fireplace, talking to his grandparents, the Cooksons, his mother's father and mother. William knew, immediately, that something was wrong.

The room had heavy velvet draperies at the window, giving it a somber look. A flickering candle on the candlestand near the bed provided the only light in the room. A highboy, dominating one wall, loomed tall and menacing to the small boy.

William listened quietly outside the room for a few minutes. Then he continued down the hall to where his sister Dorothy and his brother John were playing in the nursery. William importantly cautioned the younger children to be quiet. He reported having overheard his father tell his grandparents that their mother had slept in a damp bed in London, and that was the reason she was not well.

Ann Wordsworth had, only a few days before, returned to her parents' home from a visit to the city of London, where she had stayed at a friend's house and had, reportedly, had the "best" bedroom. Even so, she seemed to have contracted pneumonia.

John continued to pull his sister and her doll around the room in his toy wagon, not quite comprehending what his brother had said. Their older brother, Richard, was off by himself in another part of the house, and the baby, Christopher, was asleep.

It was their father's anguished sobs just an hour later that brought William, Dorothy, and John running from the nursery to see what was the matter. They listened mutely as their stunned father told them gently that their mother was dead. Two days later, on March 11, 1778, the five Wordsworth children stood together as their mother's coffin was carried out of their grandfather's house and laid to rest in the little churchyard in Penrith. The happiness and conviviality of the Wordsworth family had come to an end. The next day father and children left the Cooksons' home and made the full day's journey by horse and carriage back to their own home in Cockermouth, thirty miles away.

Before his mother's death, William Wordsworth had been a high-spirited, happy little boy of seven who was particularly close to his sister Dorothy. He had fair hair, deep-set blue eyes, small but far apart, and a dimple in his chin that softened his otherwise strong face. His nose was large, his lips full, his forehead broad rather than high. While he was far from handsome, the slight indication of sly humor that was always apparent in his eyes made him extremely attractive.

William and Dorothy had been born in a large, stately house in Cockermouth, in the north fringe of the Lake District in northern England. Cockermouth was a small, clean town, not at all the cosmopolitan marketplace that Penrith was. The Derwent River, which flowed through the town, passed over a bed of blue slate, giving its waters a steely sparkle that William always loved. The area was somewhat remote from London, which was the hub of activity in England and perhaps one of the most colorful and exciting cities in Europe at that time. Roads for traveling were extremely poor, and surrounded as they were by picturesque and peaceful countryside, the Wordsworths were not yet touched by the impending collapse of the first British Empire. This was the time that the colonists in America had decided to break away from the authority of Great Britain and to declare themselves free and independent states. The American War, as the Revolutionary War was called in England, was then in progress.

The Wordsworth house was situated on High Street, the wide, main street of Cockermouth. The house was large, square, and pretentious. As it stood, proud and cold in appearance, looking down upon the smaller and more humble houses around it, it took on an almost manorial air. It was a two-story brick-and-stone building whose central feature was five steps leading up to a beautiful doorway. A stone wall with a simple but lovely wooden gate surrounded the house.

The house opened at the back onto a garden. The River Derwent flowed past the garden, past the privet hedge and the roses, beyond the terrace. Dorothy, who was born on Christmas Day, 1771, was just twenty months younger than William, who was born on April 7, 1770. She was his constant companion and playmate here, as they swam together in the backwater of the river, looked for flowers and birds' nests with blue sparrows' eggs, and chased butterflies. Perhaps their greatest joy was exploring the moldering ruins of a feudal castle nearby at Cockermouth. Here they would clutch each other's hands and together descend into the darkness of the dungeon, and then climb out again along the old red stone walls. From here they could see the surrounding moorlands and plan their escapades for the following day. Dorothy was always eager to follow William anywhere, and together they found much joy in the sights and sounds of nature.

Shy and quiet John, a year younger than Dorothy, was too young to accompany them on all their adventures. He did tag along sometimes, though, happy just to be with his brother and sister, whom he adored and who, in turn, loved him. Richard never seemed to share their love of the out-of-doors, but spent much time playing with them at such indoor sports as tops, whist, loo, and other card games.

There was no industry in Cockermouth. Rather, this little town was a center for sheep and wool trade. The children were often left to themselves and allowed to roam freely about the picturesque countryside, wandering over the heaths and playing in the woods to their hearts' content, free from any cares.

The three middle children's delight in nature was probably the greatest inheritance of their childhood, for their love of nature continued as they became adults. It was Dorothy's recollection (twenty-five years later) of their delight as children in butterflies that prompted her brother to write:

> Oh! pleasant, pleasant were the days,
> The time, when in our childish plays,
> My sister Emmeline and I
> Together chased the butterfly!
>
> A very hunter did I rush
> Upon the prey:—with leaps and springs
> I followed on from brake to bush;
> But she, God love her! feared to brush
> The dust from off its wings.

When not delighting in the joys of the outdoors, William could be found with a book in his hands. He read much from his father's great library, but also "hoarded up" his own scanty funds to buy his own books. He loved to lose himself in fairy tales or tales of heroic legends, a favorite of which was *Arabian Nights.* Once he took his little yellow canvas-covered abridged copy of *Arabian Nights* on a fishing expedition, only to forget about the rod, line, and fish as he lay for hours on the warm, dry stones by the river, reading.

Their father, John Wordsworth, was an attorney and

the law agent, or business manager, for Sir James Lowther, the most powerful man in Cumberland County. In this capacity it was necessary for John Wordsworth to be away from home quite often, for his job entailed managing all the Lowther affairs. He provided well for his family, though, and when he was home, he encouraged William to read and to learn by heart "large portions of Shakespeare, Milton and Spenser." He himself was intelligent, well read, and an eloquent speaker. Although he was a respected attorney and a prosperous man, John Wordsworth was a member of the English middle class, not of the local gentry. Despite his position, the family lived simply and plainly.

William's mother, Ann, to whom the job of rearing her children had fallen completely, had been a gentle soul who had quietly taught her children right from wrong, but who loved them, trusted their natural instincts, and allowed them much freedom. It was she who taught them to read before they went to school, and was to them "the heart and hinge of all our learning and our loves."

Ann was an exceptional mother for her day. Families in eighteenth-century England were large, and mothers whose nerves were frayed by continual childbearing often considered their children nuisances and left their upbringing to nannies. Children were dressed in tight and uncomfortable clothes and shut up indoors in stuffy rooms for most of the week. Their mothers rarely allowed them out for fear of their getting wet or dirty or tearing their clothes. Not so Ann Wordsworth.

Ann adored her children and spent much time and care on their well-being and their education. Both she and her husband were aware of their children's fine qualities—of their inborn gifts of intelligence and sensitivity—and rejected any temptations to stifle these. A "spirit of light" existed inside the austere brick house in Cockermouth, and the Wordsworth children benefited greatly. To her children Ann was truly a mother hen who

> doth she little more
> Than move with them in tenderness and love,
> A center to the circle which they make.

Their Cookson grandparents, Ann's mother and father, disappproved of this breakdown in the old tradition of formality and strictness, and they attempted to instill some discipline into the children on their regular long visits to Penrith.

Since Ann died when William was only seven years old, his recollections of her were few and vague, but he never forgot her pinning a nosegay on his jacket before he went to church one Easter.

Shortly after her death, the distraught John Wordsworth found that he could not cope with a family of five active, growing children, the big house in Cockermouth, and his job for Sir James. Accordingly, he decided to send Dorothy to her mother's cousin, Miss Elizabeth Threlkeld, in Halifax, and the boys to their Cookson grandparents at Penrith.

Dorothy was well loved and cared for in Halifax and

relatively happy with her young cousins, the children of Miss Threlkeld's dead sister, Mrs. Ferguson, but she was sad at not being able to remain with her brothers.

The boys were anything but happy, for the Cooksons' house was a stern one. The Cooksons themselves were strict, staid, prosperous people who objected to the free and easygoing life of their daughter's children. They owned a house and shop at the north end of the market square in Penrith. Mr. Cookson was a mercer—a dealer in linen cloth—and interested in little else. The Cooksons worked in the house and the shop six days a week, going out only on Sundays. Their house was a silent one, their only conversation revolving around work. No tenderness or affection was ever apparent there.

Mrs. Cookson had been Dorothy Crackanthorpe of Newbiggin Hall before her marriage to William Cookson of Penrith. Hers was a very ancient family and one distinguished in the annals of learning. Thus the Wordsworth children came by their intelligence naturally. They were descended from an intellectual and aristocratic family. Their early milieu was bourgeois, however, and all through their lives they maintained a democratic attitude that seemed out of touch with Newbiggin Hall and all it implied.

The Cooksons, in their attempt to counteract their grandsons' lack of discipline, found fault with them constantly and scolded them continuously, making them feel even more acutely the loss of their mother.

William, already a fearless and defiant child by the age of eight, became even more stubborn and rebellious under this treatment. The punishments he received seemed only to increase his defiance. In fact, the incorrigible little boy often antagonized his grandparents deliberately and seemed proud of the punishments he provoked. As ringleader of the group, he was often beaten, ignored by his Uncle Christopher, his mother's brother, insulted by the servants, and not spoken to at all by his grandfather. But William was undaunted. There seemed to be something within him that was driving him, some inner force that compelled him to rebel against his grandparents, against the fixed and proper routine of life in their house.

One day, while whipping tops with his brother Richard in an upstairs drawing room whose walls were hung with family portraits, he said to his brother, "Dare you strike your whip through that old lady's petticoat?"

"No, I won't," said the cautious and obedient Richard.

"Then here goes!" And William did the deed himself, destroying the canvas, then waiting to hear his grandfather's step on the stairs, knowing full well that he would be severely beaten.

On another occasion, in a fit of violent temper, he stormed to the attic, threatening suicide. He planned to destroy himself with one of the foils that he knew were kept there. He took the sword in hand, pointed it toward his heart, then lost his courage.

He seemed to be fulfilling the undesirable aspect of his mother's earlier prophecy that he would be remarkable either for good or for evil. She had, in fact, once confided to a friend that William was the only one of her children whose future gave her cause for concern.

There were a few happy spots of time in William's

otherwise dreary days at Penrith, when he was at the small dame school where Mrs. Ann Birkett, a kind old lady, taught him the basics of reading, writing, and arithmetic, and encouraged him to read. Dame schools, so called because they were taught by respect-worthy women, or dames, were popular in England at this time.

The main teaching tool used in dame schools—besides the rod—was the hornbook. This was not actually a book. Rather, it was a sheet of paper with the alphabet in capital and small letters, Roman numerals, and the Lord's Prayer printed on it. This sheet was mounted on a thin piece of wood about nine by five inches and covered with transparent horn for protection. (Horn is the hard, smooth material forming the outer covering of the horns of cattle.) The edges were bound with metal, and on the back was a colored picture. One hornbook, "published" by gingerbread bakers, was extremely popular with children. They could eat each letter as they learned its name.

Mrs. Birkett did not believe in taxing the reasoning powers of her young pupils, but taught them instead to learn by rote, having them memorize portions of the Bible. In her classroom William soon became friendly with a quiet, plain, but cheerful little girl named Mary Hutchinson, who lived in Penrith and was to become important to him many years later.

Chapter 2

My Heart Leaps Up

A little less than two years after their mother's death, William, Richard, and John were finally able to escape the unhappy life with their grandparents. They were sent to live with "Dame" Ann and Hugh Tyson in the tiny hamlet of Colthouse, thirty miles away, and a whole day's journey by horse southeast from Cockermouth. The boys were to attend the Hawkshead Grammar School in Hawkshead, half a mile west of Colthouse.

Hawkshead School was one of the many grammar schools that had sprung up in England in the sixteenth century as a result of the religious reformation and the revival of an interest in learning. It had been founded in 1585, during the reign of Queen Elizabeth, by Edwin Sandys, then Archbishop of York.

While the school was primarily attended by local farmers' sons who planned to enter the clergy, its reputation was so high during the second half of the eighteenth century, when William and his brothers were there, that boys came from great distances to attend. These were sons not only of farmers but of local gentry, clergy, and professional men. Free instruction was given to the children of the district, but those who did not live in the Lake District paid a "cock-penny" or entrance fee of a guinea a year—about five dollars then, but the equivalent of about fifty dollars today. This was quite different from the "public" schools, which were, in fact, private in the American sense, and attended only by the aristocracy because of the large fees charged.

The Hawkshead school, still standing today, is a small and modest stone building just down the street from the church and adjoining the village graveyard, a favorite playground of the boys after school. It is hard to distinguish the school building from the cottages that surround it. Inside, a visitor can readily identify the desk where William sat by his initials, which he carved in it so many years ago.

The boys at Hawkshead were taught by a headmaster and an usher, or teacher. The headmasters were all graduates of Cambridge University, and had been ordained in the Church of England. Thus, they were all Anglican clergymen.

The boys studied Latin, the elements of Greek, the mathematics of Euclid, and the classics, particularly the works of Ovid, Virgil, and Homer. They read much English poetry. Mr. William Taylor, the headmaster from 1782 until 1786, also helped them to become acquainted with names such as Francis Bacon and Sir Isaac Newton, and with the more scientific approach to knowledge that was just becoming popular. Perhaps more diversified studies were offered in other schools, but Hawkshead was considered one of the best in the North.

The school would today be considered very old-fashioned, but it did have many advantages. It was one of the most liberal schools of its day. There were no organized athletics, nor was there competition or pressure. It was known for its scholarship and for the free and happy life led by its boys. They were never beaten. In fact, there was no brutality there, as there was at many of the public schools. Soon William's days became as happy as his days in Cockermouth had been before his mother's death.

By our standards the school day would seem extremely long. In summer the boys attended from six o'clock until eleven in the morning, and from one until five in the afternoon. In winter, when the days were shorter, classes were from seven to eleven, and from twelve thirty until four o'clock. These hours, however, included time for individual study, so the boys had no homework and were completely free after school. They were free to roam the countryside and to enjoy this dramatically beautiful part of England. They might wander around any of its dozen lakes, its four mountains and many lower hills and rocky crags, its crystal-clear smaller ponds, its meadows and woodlands.

William did well in his studies of the classics and mathematics, and retained a love of the Latin classics all his life. He read Virgil's *Aeneid* in Latin and parts of Homer's *Iliad* in Greek. Years later William could read Latin easily at sight, but he generally read Greek authors in translation. Even when he was very young, he had a burning desire to learn. He took great delight in discovering every day something fresh and new in his world. But it was books that he loved and wanted most. He would read all kinds of books—fairy tales that sparked his imagination when he was very young, then, at school, tours and travel, histories and biographies, and, of course, poetry. He read all of Henry Fielding's works and much of Jonathan Swift, whose *Gulliver's Travels* and *A Tale of a Tub* were among his favorites. He liked and imitated the style of Alexander Pope, but loved and revered most of all the great poet John Milton. William also enjoyed the Romantic poets—the "modern" poets of his day— Robert Burns, James Beattie, and Thomas Chatterton, a brilliant young poet whose career began in his midteens and ended tragically with his suicide when he was eighteen.

William was not alone in his love of reading. The educated in eighteenth-century England had a tremendous interest in reading. Though small, the reading public had a high standard of taste. To the Georgian Englishman (so called because England at that time was ruled by George III), poetry and literature were almost a necessity of life. Paperbacks flourished at this time, and these inexpensive and convenient pocket volumes were within the reach of most middle- and upper-class people, making reading one of their common pleasures.

It was a time of much writing as well as reading. Newspapers and periodicals abounded. Poetry had been written for centuries, but the modern English novel was born in eighteenth-century England, when Samuel Richardson wrote *Pamela*. Poetry, however, remained the foremost literary form of the day. Everybody tried his hand at writing poetry. In fact, during William's life the novel was considered a bourgeois form.

William's "dame" at Colthouse, Ann Tyson, no doubt made a modest profit from her boarders, but she seems to have loved them all and to have treated them as if they were the children she never had. She was also what we would refer to today as a dressmaker. With much woolen cloth at home for the women of Hawkshead to choose from, she made skirts and gowns to order. She also sold some stockings and handkerchiefs, although many people wore woolen stockings that they had knitted at home.

Hugh Tyson, Ann's husband, was a joiner by trade. Joiners were men skilled in securing pieces of wood to one another without the use of nails, somewhat like the interlocking pieces of a jigsaw puzzle. It was in the English tradition of joinery that many beautiful cupboards, chests, and clock cases were made. Hugh sometimes made clogwheels for the carts used in the Lake District and wooden troughs for carrying water. Joiners were also called upon to mend a cradle or to make a coffin or a yoke for a team of oxen.

Greenend, as the Tyson's cottage was called, was built about 1700, and is situated a few yards back from the road in what was once a small, open square but is now an enclosed garden. It was long and narrow, with five rooms downstairs and five or six bedrooms upstairs. In William's room a visitor today can still see his name carved in the window seat: Wm. Wordsworth. At the back of the house was a courtyard surrounded by several outbuildings, one of which was probably Hugh's workshop. In front of the house was a garden with a pine tree and a stone table at which the Tysons, William, and his brothers and friends often sat. A noisy little brook flowed through the garden.

William was now living the carefree, happy life of a schoolboy, marred only by the sadness of not having his sister Dorothy with him. Their letters to each other, however, and his vivid memory allowed him to keep her image strong.

Hawkshead was nestled among the hills of High Furness, in the shallow valley of Esthwaite, at the northwest corner of the lake of Esthwaite Water. With its sprinkling of small farms and its woodlands of hazel and birch and oak trees spreading wildly over the hills above, it soon became the scene of many exciting adventures for him.

He spent much time with his friends in active sports, but often went off by himself, climbing the great cliffs of Coniston Old Man or Wetherlam in search of ravens' nests, looting them for the sheer joy of it, setting snares for woodcocks who came in large numbers on winter migrations, and often even stealing woodcocks from traps set by others. He was barely ten years old when he spent half a night setting springes, or traps, for birds in the mountains, running back and forth among them to see if he had caught any. But when

> . . . the bird
> Which was the captive of another's toil
> Became my prey; and when the deed was done
> I heard among the solitary hills
> Low breathings coming after me, and sounds
> Of undistinguishable motion, steps
> Almost as silent as the turf they trod.

Immediately, William became remorseful and frightened. He, the son of an estate manager, must have known that poaching, killing game or fish illegally, was a serious crime. But the thrill of what he was doing seems to have outweighed his feelings of guilt and his fear, for he continued.

> . . . though mean
> Our object and inglorious, yet the end
> Was not ignoble. Oh! when I have hung
> Above the raven's nest . . .
>   . . .
> While on the perilous ridge I hung alone,
> With what strange utterance did the loud, dry wind
> Blow through my ear! The sky seemed not a sky
> Of earth—and with what motion moved the clouds!

One day, sometime after his arrival at Hawkshead, just after school let out one afternoon, William left his friends outside the schoolhouse and wandered off by himself. Despite the wildly blowing wind and rain, he ambled through the hollows and over the cliffs of the valley of Coniston. His perceptive eyes took in the patchwork quilt of the landscape spread out below him, the smooth green pastures on the shores of Coniston Water, the cattle huddled together there and the impressive peaks of Coniston Old Man and Wetherlam, towering above him. As he watched the blue-gray smoke curling up from the slate quarries below, the scene was imprinted permanently on his mind.

Suddenly the rain stopped, and a rainbow appeared, bridging the valley and, incredibly, remaining visible for several minutes. Many years later, in the spring of 1802, the memory of that unusual rainbow was still with him, and prompted him to write:

> My heart leaps up when I behold
> A rainbow in the sky:
> So was it when my life began;
> So is it now I am a man;
> So be it when I shall grow old,
> > Or let me die!

As he walked home through the mountains that day, the air became noisy with the sound of running water and the sun burst through the clouds so that, as he approached Hawkshead, that quaint and quiet village was illuminated in the bright sunshine.

He saw the modest gray stone houses of the village, with their thick-slabbed slate roofs, set in a haphazard yet charming manner around several irregularly shaped squares. The houses had a homely feeling of comfort about them. William particularly enjoyed the view of the ancient church. A long gray mass rising abruptly from one side of the village, the church was difficult to distinguish from the rock on which it rested, so naturally did it blend into its surroundings in shape and color. In fact, the church and the houses seemed almost to have grown right out of the materials around them.

When he entered Greenend, William was still profoundly moved by what he had just experienced. He was grateful to Ann for not commenting on his wet clothes or how late he was for dinner.

On a night such as this the "family" may have been eating leg of mutton for dinner and "kek" for dessert. The kek was a rare treat of mince pie made in large rounds and nearly two inches thick. William no doubt thought how lucky he was to be living with Ann, whose simple affection and accepting attitude supplied him with the comfort and security he needed now his mother was dead. Ann rarely questioned any of "her boys" and received in turn their respect and love.

After dinner William, his brothers Richard and John, and Thomas Gawthorp, another lodger, often gathered around Ann in front of the peat fire and begged her to tell them again and again of her days in Scotland. Happily, Ann would comply, telling them long, detailed, often pathetic stories of people and places she had known. The boys knew that Ann had lived in Bonaw, on the River Awe, in Argyllshire, Scotland, for many years. She had been the housekeeper for the Knott family there. One of their favorite stories was how, after everyone else had been unsuccessful, Ann had got little George Knott to eat his porridge by making it very thick and spreading honey on top. Then, coming to work for George Knott many years later when he was a married man and a father, she found that he still ate his porridge that way.

Ann told sad stories also. She told the boys of the early death of Mary Rigge. Mary had been a young friend of Ann. She was deserted by a gentleman in the neighborhood just before she gave birth to his child, whom she named David Benoni, or "child of sorrow." Mary died, presumably of a broken heart, one year later at the age of twenty-one.

Ann told the boys also about a shepherd and his son and their search for a missing sheep in the highlands. She told them the simple tale of an old shepherd, Michael, of his deep love for his only son, Luke, and his despair at losing him in a desperate effort to save his land. The old man had sent his beloved son to the city to earn the money needed to save the land, but Luke "gave himself to evil causes" there and eventually had to run away and hide across the sea.

William listened eagerly as she spun her yarns, and his keen memory and vivid imagination were to transform these into beautiful ballads many years later. He paid tribute to the source of these poems when he wrote:

> It was the first
> Of those domestic tales that spake to me
> Of shepherds, dwellers in the valleys, men
> Whom I already loved; not verily
> For their own sakes, but for the fields and hills
> Where was their occupation and abode.
> And hence this Tale, while I was yet a Boy.

Chapter 3

With All the Sorrow

William and his brothers Richard and John had been at Hawkshead about four years when they were struck by the next major tragedy of their lives. They had become reasonably happy there, were loved and cared for by Ann, respectful of, yet friendly, with their masters at school, on happy terms with all the inhabitants of the area—the boatman who drove his ferry back and forth across Lake Windermere, the shepherds, the villagers, even the old beggars and the wandering packmen, those wonderful journeymen who carried in their backpacks the many wares unobtainable in the tiny villages.

As happy as they had become at Hawkshead, however, the boys always looked forward eagerly to their holidays at home in Cockermouth. These meant reunion with their father and Christopher (who was still considered too young to join them at school and was living, save for the holidays, with their grandparents at Penrith), and occasional visits to their Uncle Richard, their father's brother in Whitehaven, just ten miles west of Cockermouth, on the Irish Sea.

Richard Wordsworth was the collector of customs

there. At Whitehaven the boys were able to play with their nine Wordsworth cousins, watch the ships come into this thriving port, and listen to tales of storms and shipwrecks. Here also William, no doubt, developed a respect for mariners that later was to carry over to his feeling for his brother John. And it was here, no doubt, that John was influenced toward a career at sea. For Whitehaven was then a flourishing port, rivaling the ports of London, Liverpool, Bristol, and Newcastle. It was important for its coal mines, shipbuilding, and the importing of tobacco from the Colony of Virginia.

When they were visiting at Whitehaven, the boys would often reminisce about how their sister Dorothy, when she was very young, had suddenly burst into tears upon seeing and hearing the sea for the first time. It became a favorite family story and was an indication of the sensitivity of this little girl.

At the start of Christmas vacation in 1783, William, now thirteen and a half, thought of all this, of seeing his father and Christopher, of possibly visiting his Uncle Richard's family at Whitehaven, but most of all of just being together with his brothers in a house where they were completely free and happy. He became more and more eager to get home. In fact, he bcame so restless and excited that impulsively he left Greenend and ran out into the fields, up to a high crag overlooking the roads by which the groom and ponies his father always sent to bring them home might be coming. It was a dark, wild, stormy day, the kind that William seemed to like best, and he sat down on the wet grass, protected only by a low stone wall. "Scoutlike," he strained his eyes whenever the mist parted enough for him to see the woods and the roads below, hoping that by watching he might bring the ponies even faster.

When he finally saw them approaching, the groom riding one pony and leading two more, William ran excitedly down the ridge and back to Colthouse, shouting to his brothers to hurry. After hasty good-byes to Ann and Hugh, they rushed back along the path, eager not to waste one precious minute. The ride home was joyful, William and Richard each riding his own pony and John, still too young to ride alone, sitting atop the third with the groom sitting behind him. They spent much of the time devising exciting plans for their long holiday. But their joy was short-lived.

When they arrived at Cockermouth, they found the household quiet and anxious. Their first indication that something was amiss was the fact that Christopher had not been brought home from Penrith. They soon learned that their father had been on a business trip just a few days before, and returning home on horseback one bitter cold evening, had lost his way in the darkness and been forced to spend the night in the mountains of Cold Fell, with no shelter available. The chill he suffered, together with his probable lack of desire to fight for his life now that his wife was gone, proved fatal. Ten days later, on a gusty, snowy day, the three Wordsworth brothers—Richard, fifteen, William, thirteen, and John, eleven—dry-eyed but awestricken, stood together once more, orphans now, as their father's coffin was carried out of the house and laid to rest in the little churchyard in Cocker-mouth. John Wordsworth had just passed his forty-second birthday.

William's immediate thought was that his father's death was punishment for his own impatience to leave for home, for his selfish wishes.

> The event
> With all the sorrow that it brought, appeared
> A chastisement; and when I called to mind
> That day so lately pass'd, when from the crag
> I looked in such anxiety of hope;
> With trite reflections of morality,
> Yet in the deepest passion, I bowed low
> To God, who thus corrected my desires.

He never forgot the picture of his wait for the ponies and, through the years,

> when storm and rain
> Beat on my roof, or, haply, at noon-day
> While in a grove I walk, whose lefty trees,
> Laden with summer's thickest foliage, rock
> In a strong wind, some working of the spirit,
> Some inward agitations thence are brought. . . .

Life could never again be the same for the Wordsworth boys. Their uncles, Richard Wordsworth and Christopher (Kit) Cookson (their mother's brother, with whom William was never able to get along), became their legal guardians. It fell to these two, and eventually to the younger Richard Wordsworth, oldest son of their father's brother, to attempt to collect from Sir James Lowther all the money he legally owed to John Wordsworth. For on John Wordsworth's death, the unscrupulous Sir James refused to pay all the back salary that he owed John Wordsworth—the very large sum of £4,700 (which was equal to about $12,000 and is the equivalent of about $50,000 today). It was not until the year 1802 that the dispute between the Wordsworth children's guardians and the Lowther descendant (for James Lowther had since died) was finally settled and the debt paid.

As the children watched the house on High Street, the grandest house they were ever to live in, being emptied and all its beautiful furnishings being sold, it was, perhaps, some consolation to William when his cousin Richard heeded his pleas that his father's books and bookcase be saved for him. These were sent to Richard's house in Branthwaite.

William had never been very close to his father. John Wordsworth's reserved manner and his long absences from home had made it difficult for his children to develop intimate relationships with him. They seemed to feel for him more respect than love. In fact, John Wordsworth seems to have made few close relationships in his lifetime: "Amongst all those who visited at my father's house he had not one real friend," Dorothy wrote years later to her friend Jane Pollard. The hardest loss for the boys, therefore, was probably the final loss of a happy home.

When the boys returned to Greenend at the close of the Christmas holidays, Christopher went with them, and soon they had settled again into the life at Hawkshead.

Chapter 4

Under Hawkshead's Happy Roof

One Monday morning, sitting around the breakfast table eating their oatmeal with brown sugar and milk, the boys made plans for a nutting expedition after school. Ann warned them to come home first and change into something old, so as not to ruin their school clothes. William mused idly that this was the only restriction Ann ever placed on them. The only time she really interfered in their lives was when she insisted on their wearing the old and ragged clothes she saved for their expeditions into the woods:

> I left our cottage threshold . . .
> . . . a figure quaint,
> Tricked out in proud disguise of cast-off weeds
>   . . .
> By exhortation of my frugal dame.

"And no wonder," he thought. He often did come home torn and disheveled after an afternoon of gathering nuts.

After breakfast the boys left Greenend and headed for school. On the way two more boys, John Fleming and

Robert Greenwood, joined their group. As they walked toward school, they passed through the marketplace and stopped to chat with an old woman as she spread her yarn on a large gray rock and prepared to offer it for sale. For this was market day in Hawkshead, and yarn was the principal product sold. Many of the families in the area spun and wove the yarn and then took the cloth by packhorse south along the narrow lanes to Kendal where they sold it.

When they started on their way again, William and John Fleming ran a little ahead of the others, hoping for a chance to see their headmaster and good friend, William Taylor. This teacher was young, scholarly, quiet—with a keen love and appreciation of the poets of his day. He communicated this enthusiasm for poetry to the boys, particularly to William. It was he who introduced William to the poetry of the young Chatterton and showed him its beauty as well as the tragedy of this poet's brief life. It was he who also introduced William to all the poets of the eighteenth century—those who had already attained fame and prominence, and those who were just beginning to write. Taylor reminded William of his own father, who had always encouraged him to read and who had kindled in him his first enthusiasm for books. Taylor, in his lovable, easygoing manner, was building now on this love of books and developing in William a taste for poetry.

Taylor had, just the week before, lent William a volume from his own library, *The Minstrel* by James Beattie, and this rustic poem had made a vivid impression on the boy. The poem traces the progress of a poetical genius from his birth until that time when he is considered a minstrel—that is, a poet and musician. William had finished it quickly, being an avid reader, and with Mr. Taylor's permission, had passed it on to John Fleming. These two were great friends. Enjoying each other's companionship, they wandered together around Esthwaite's shores and recited poetry to one another, illustrating the old adage that reading poetry aloud was once part of the Englishness of the English.

Each of the boys found in the other a happy companion for racing boats and skating, their favorite sport, as well as a kindred spirit for enjoying the beauties of nature and poetry. William was at one time so full of youthful love for his friend that he was moved to write: "Friendship and Fleming are the same."

That morning Mr. Taylor welcomed the two boys enthusiastically and told William that he had a very special little book for him to borrow, one that had recently been given to him as a gift. The volume was Chatterton's *Miscellanies in Prose and Verse.* Several years later, when William was writing verses at school, he quoted from the poetry of Thomas Chatterton.

How lucky William was to have been at Hawkshead and to have had Mr. Taylor as a headmaster and a friend. For Taylor was a remarkable man and a remarkable educator for his time. It was he who often "heard" the younger boys in their reading and helped them with their lessons. It was he who allowed William the freedom to indulge his habit of wandering. And his gentle guidance of the young poet was one of the most important influences on William.

Mr. Taylor seems to have recognized the budding talent

in William and to have communicated his confidence in him as a poet to the boy. He inspired William not only to read the modern poets of the day, but to try his own hand at writing. Indeed, William's first surviving attempt at writing poetry (at the age of fifteen) had been at William Taylor's urging—as an assignment celebrating the bicentennial of the school. "Under Hawkshead's happy roof," he wrote,

> There have I loved to show the tender age
> The golden precepts of the classic page;
> To lead the mind to those Elysian plains
> Where, throned in gold, immortal Science reigns.

But he was even younger ("thirteen years or haply less") when he first became conscious of loving "words in tuneful order" and

> . . . found them sweet
> For their own sakes, a passion and a power.

In fact, he may have first experienced this love of words when he was just a small boy reading books from his father's great library in the old house in Cockermouth that he had loved and that he remembered so well.

Although they have not survived, William wrote his first voluntary verses during the Christmas season of 1784–1785, the year following his father's death. The boys were spending their holiday with their Uncle Richard Wordsworth at Whitehaven. William, always an enthusiastic dancer, even at the age of fourteen, had walked six miles to attend a dance at Egremont and had then composed a poem. Shortly thereafter he was given as a gift a brown leather manuscript book in which he began to compose verses. He took this book with him when he went to Cambridge three years later, and continued to write in it for many years.

After school that Monday afternoon, as they had planned at breakfast, William, John, and Thomas Gawthorp, who also lodged with the Tysons, changed into their old clothes and set off for the hazel woods. They each had a huge wallet, a cloth pouch at the end of a long stick, slung over one shoulder, and a nutting crook —a stick with a bent end, rather like an old man's walking cane—in hand. In the woods they took their crooks and roughly "dragged to earth both branch and bough," excitedly filling their bags with their bounty of nuts. At the time William could think of little that would give him greater pleasure. To gather hazelnuts in the woods and then return home made him feel "exulting, rich beyond the wealth of kings."

On half-holidays from school William, his brothers, and John Fleming often went skating and boating with their Hawkshead schoolmates. They would leave the quiet of the valley of Esthwaite, walk four miles over a ridge of hills to Bowness ferry on the spectacularly beautiful Lake Windermere, rent boats, and race to one of the islands off Bowness. Perhaps their favorite occupation was to row to the inn on the Bowness shore, where they could then spend hours bowling on the green adjacent to the magnificent inn and later, feeling very elegant indeed, treat themselves to strawberries and cream inside its great doors.

On other occasions, when they had some money, they would rent horses (taking care not to admit how far they planned to take them) and ride to the red sandstone ruins of the abbey church at Furness more than twenty miles away. It was probably quite late at night before they returned from these escapades, but it was in the dark and gloom of the nave of Furness Abbey that William heard the song of a "single wren:"

> So sweetly 'mid the gloom the invisible Bird
> Sang to herself, that there I could have made
> My dwelling place, and liv'd for ever there
> To hear such music.

In winter their favorite sport was skating on the lake, and often they stayed out until well after dark, ignoring the many calls to come home for dinner:

> . . . happy time
> It was indeed for all of us—for me
> It was a time of rapture! Clear and loud
> The village clock tolled six,—I wheeled about,
> Proud and exulting like an untired horse
> That cares not for his home. All shod with steel,
> We hissed along the polished ice in games confederate.
>   . . .
> So through the darkness and the cold we flew
> And not a voice was idle; with the din
> Smitten, the precipices rang aloud;

> The leafless trees and every icy crag
> Tinkled like iron; . . .

Organized, competitive games were not a part of life at Hawkshead.

Sometimes, very early in the morning, well before it was time to leave for school, William would quietly lift the latch on the cottage door, slip out to meet John, and walk with him the five miles around the shores of Esthwaite Lake.

> Here,
> . . . Amid the sweep of endless woods,
> Blue pomp of lakes, high cliffs, and falling floods.

Before any smoke had risen from the cottages or the birds had begun to sing, they would sit in the woods watching the slumbering valley greet the first light of dawn.

Occasionally William would wander through the dales by himself and visit with families in the cottages. He was a friendly youngster, and they always welcomed him warmly. He enjoyed seeing how the entire family worked together spinning and carding wool. Even the old grandfather, no longer able to work in the field, helped. "Often, when a boy, have I admired the cylinders of carded wool which were softly laid upon each other by his side," William wrote years later.

He loved also to watch the yarn and cloth being loaded onto the backs of packhorses to be taken from the farms along the narrow lanes to Hawkshead, and then on south

45

to Kendal to be sold. These rough roads were bordered on each side by irregularly shaped gray stones of varying sizes, placed seemingly at random, one atop the other, to form the charming stone walls that still line the country lanes of England.

All these scenes were indelibly imprinted on William's mind. Years later, as a grown man, he could conjure up images of his life at Hawkshead and transfer these into simple and beautiful poetry. He had seen with the keen intensity of a young boy; it was his gift that he never lost this ability. It was this same ability to retain images that permitted him to keep his sister Dorothy fresh in his mind for the many years they were apart.

In 1786 William and John Fleming, together with several of the "upper" boys, were summoned to William Taylor's bedside, where he lay ill, and with great sorrow heard him say, "My head will soon lie low." And, indeed, just a few days later their beloved headmaster, who had inspired and encouraged young William, was gone.

Eight years later a visit to his grave could still bring tears to William's eyes and move him to write:

> He loved the Poets and if now alive
> Would have loved me as one not destitute
> Of promise nor belying the kind hope
> Which he had form'd, when I at his command
> Began to spin, at first, my toilsome songs.

But inspiration and encouragement for William did not die with Mr. Taylor. Thomas Bowman, who became headmaster shortly after Mr. Taylor's death, seems to have continued to make books from his own personal library available to William and the other boys.

One afternoon when William was about sixteen years old, he went to Mr. Bowman's study to return two books that he had borrowed, *The Task,* by William Cowper, and Robert Burns's *Poems.* These had recently been published and were among those which Mr. Bowman had received that month. The latest books were sent to him every month from Kendal, and he often passed these on to William.

This afternoon the headmaster suggested to William that he look for another book to borrow while Mr. Bowman went out for a few minutes to attend to something. The headmaster was unexpectedly detained for half an hour. When he returned, William was so engrossed in a book he had discovered that he had no idea how much time had elapsed—nor did he even notice the headmaster's return. The book was Sir Isaac Newton's *Optics.*

Chapter 5

She Gave Me Eyes,
She Gave Me Ears

William's separation from his sister Dorothy lasted nine
years, until Dorothy returned to Penrith from Halifax in
the summer of 1787, and William, now seventeen, and
their brothers came "home" from Hawkshead for the
holidays. Dorothy, now fifteen years old, arrived first and
was immediately put to work in her grandparents' house
and in their shop. It was not long before she found herself terribly unhappy, longing for the warmth of her
cousin's bustling household in Halifax, the companionship of her friend there, Jane Pollard, but most of all
eagerly looking forward to the return of her brothers.

As she sat for hours silently mending old shirts for her
grandmother, selling textile fabrics in the shop, or listening to her grandmother's lectures on the necessity of
being docile and sedate, she tried hard to stifle her own
naturally warm, affectionate, and impetuous nature.
As this child, who had reveled in the out-of-doors, miser-
ably watched the sunshine that she was allowed to enjoy

only on Sundays, she felt more and more like a caged bird. In a rare moment of freedom she wrote to Jane:

> One would imagine that a grandmother would feel for her grandchild all the tenderness of a mother, particularly when that grandchild had no other parent, but there is so little of tenderness in her manner or of anything affectionate, that while I am in her house I cannot at all consider myself as at home, I feel like a stranger. We sit for hours without saying anything.

William, still at Hawkshead, was also waiting eagerly for his reunion with his sister. As he and his brothers watched each day for the arrival of the horses to carry them home, waking up each morning and thinking, "Today will be the day!" he became more and more apprehensive. He remembered only too well another time when he had been impatient for their arrival. Finally, frantic with anxiety, after having waited an entire week, he left Richard, John, and Christopher waiting at Colthouse and hired his own horse to take him to Penrith. He had become fearful that someone might be ill there.

When William arrived at Penrith, he discovered that the horses had not been sent because he had not mentioned them specifically in his letter, but had only stated when school would close. The fact that this had always been sufficient in the past was ignored. Dorothy, in a letter to Jane Pollard, blamed this on the "ill-nature" of her Uncle Kit Cookson.

The reunion of the brothers and their sister was, nonetheless, joyous. Instantly, it was as if William and Dorothy had never been apart. These two spent every free moment together, Dorothy often having to steal away from the tasks her grandmother always had for her. Together they rambled through the countryside and reminisced about Cockermouth in the ruins of nearby Brougham Castle, where they lay on top of the tower in the sunshine listening to the sounds of summer. The charm and melancholy of ruins such as Cockermouth and Brougham castles and of Furness Abbey sparked William's romantic imagination. Here also they read the poetry of the new, young Scottish poet Robert Burns. Later, William was to write that he had learned from Burns:

> How verse may build a princely throne
> On humble truth.

William celebrated the great joy of his companionship with Dorothy in the very beautiful lines:

> The blessings of my later years
> Was with me when a boy:
> She gave me eyes, she gave me ears:
> And humble cares, and delicate fears;
> A heart, the fountain of sweet tears;
> And love, and thought, and joy.

At seventeen, William had finally learned to ignore his grandparents and his Uncle Kit. They had become to him no more than the disagreeable characters he had met in the fairy tales he read when just a little boy.

William and Dorothy also had a chance to renew their friendship with Mary Hutchinson, William's friend of his earlier dame-school days in Penrith. Mary and Dorothy were the same age, and they found they had much in common. Soon the three became an inseparable group.

But the peaceful quality of life in northern England was soon to be dispelled. In a short time their entire world—this peaceful and prosperous country life—would vanish and a new world would be created before their eyes. The American Revolution had robbed England of her "white empire" in the West, while she was, at the same time, gaining India in the East.

Perhaps even more important, the Industrial Revolution was just beginning in England. The population was steadily increasing. Roads were being built, supplemented by canals, making transportation between the North and South of England easier. There was at the time an increasing use of the square-rigger, a sailing vessel allowing the merchant fleet greater mobility and, therefore, giving trade with India a chance to grow. Manufacturing was on the increase. James Hargreaves' spinning jenny was first used in the cottages in 1765, and in 1769 Richard Arkwright had patented his spinning frame and erected the first practical cotton mill in the world. Thus, the factory system came into being, and the cottage textile industry as it was carried on in Penrith and in Hawkshead was slowly ending. Soon cotton spinning would be taken out of the cottage workshop away from the women and children and into the mills. The full-time employment of villagers in such trades as clock making, tanning, basket weaving, wagon building, tailoring, and the great national industry of cloth weaving would soon come to an end. The rural quality of life would vanish, and the modern industrial world would come into being. Now, for the first time since Anglo-Saxon days, Northumbria was to regain the important position it had held until the middle of the seventh century. For the Industrial Revolution was to make the coal and iron resources of the North more valuable than the cornfields of the South and East. Perhaps, even then, unconsciously, William, Dorothy, and Mary were seeking refuge in nature from the industry that was springing up around them.

Chapter 6

What Holy Joy
There Is in Knowledge

As the summer of 1787 drew near its end, so also did the brief reunion of William and Dorothy, for their grandparents and their Uncle Kit Cookson insisted that, rather than remain at Penrith for the month of September, William return to Hawkshead with his brothers John and Christopher before leaving for Cambridge, where he was to begin studying that fall.

Early in October 1787, William, now seventeen and a half, finally took leave of Ann and Hugh Tyson, his younger brothers (Richard was already attending Cambridge), and his beloved vale of Esthwaite, and returned to Penrith for three weeks to prepare for his trip to Cambridge. Here he met his Uncle William Cookson, a clergyman and fellow of St. John's College, Cambridge. William Cookson was a kind and affectionate man, not at all like his brother Kit, and he was eager to guide and help both William and Dorothy. They responded to him immediately. Dorothy wrote of him to Jane Pollard:

I am now writing beside that uncle I so much love. . . . Every day gives me new proof of his affection, and every day I like him better than I did before. I am now with him two hours every morning, from nine till eleven. I then read and write French, and learn arithmetic. When I am a good arithmetician I am to learn geography. I sit in his room when we have a fire. He knows I am often pinched for time when I write [letters] so he told me I might do that instead of my French. . . . I had my brother William with me for three weeks. I was very busy during his stay preparing him for Cambridge.

When, on the twenty-third of October, William finally set out for Cambridge, he was dressed in the new clothes Dorothy had sewed for him and was accompanied by his Uncle William and his cousin, John Myers, who was also headed for St. John's. The three men traveled by coach from Penrith to Cambridge. They made the journey in seven days, including a brief stopover in York, considered then the capital of the North. As they approached the medieval city of York, they were struck by the awesome and beautiful York Minster, the cathedral looming in the distance, its white stone walls seeming to dominate the landscape.

Weary from their journey, William, John, and their uncle stopped for a few days to rest and visit with John Myers' married sister, who lived in York. Several days later, feeling rested and refreshed after their brief respite, but eager to be in Cambridge, the three set forth again on the last leg of their journey. They traveled by chaise over difficult roads across sprawling fields and woodlands, through the sometimes treacherous moors that were just then beginning to be enclosed by stone walls, fences, and hedges.

Traveling then was extremely hazardous. Roads were narrow, darkened by overgrown trees, and intersected by ruts. During a dry summer, travelers were often blinded by clouds of dust. Then, after a heavy rainfall, roads became an impassable gulf of mud. During the fall, when William, John, and their uncle were traveling, there were often deep ruts full of water, with hard, dry ridges that made it almost impossible for the coaches to cross. Overturning of coaches was very common. The three were fortunate, however, that they were not stopped by a highwayman along the way, for the fear of being robbed or beaten by these "knights of the road" was great in eighteenth-century England. Any long journey was an unpleasant and frightening undertaking.

They continued south via the Great North Road through the industrial town of Nottingham in the Midlands and then on through the little towns of Stamford, Huntingdon, and Saint Ives. Finally, on October 30, 1787, King's College Chapel, with its great windows of sixteenth-century glass, suddenly appeared on the horizon. Minutes later they were crossing the Magdalene Bridge over the sunlit, sleepy River Cam, so lovely, yet so different from the Derwent River. Soon they were walking on the thick green grass within the courtyard, and looking at the mellow pink brick of St. John's College, the magnificence of all the buildings, the beauty of the weeping willow trees. William's heart quickened as they passed a young Cambridge student dressed in the traditional cap and gown, and he thought with eager anticipation that he, too, would soon be studying at this university that had given the "divine Milton" to England and from which his dear William Taylor had come.

William saw very quickly an indication of Sir Isaac Newton's influence on Cambridge as he walked across the scientist's experimental wooden bridge linking the Cloister Court to Queens' College. It was constructed solely of pieces of wood fitted together. No iron had been used. Learning and applying the discoveries of Newton was then one of the chief occupations of graduates and undergraduates at Cambridge.

During the next few days William was busy but happy. He found his old friends from Hawkshead days, Robert Greenwood and John Fleming, who had come to Cambridge two years before, and Thomas Gawthorp, who had lodged with him at Ann Tyson's and was to be a freshman like himself. There were many other "North country" boys there, and William soon found himself part of a large group.

He was caught up in the bustle of getting ready for the beginning of the academic year. He bought books. He went to the tailor to order his gown, knee breeches, and white stockings. He spent money. Suddenly, he found himself transformed from a mountain youth to a college sophisticate. As he relinquished his homespun country clothes for the more elaborate college silks, ruffles, and embroidery that were then the fashion, he felt a stirring of excitement within him: "I was the dreamer, they the dream."

But his excitement and happy anticipation were to be

short-lived. William soon became disillusioned. He found himself longing for the loveliness of his northern hills, confused and silently rebellious at what he considered the hypocrisy of his fellow students. That streak of obstinacy and rebellion which had been so evident when he was a boy at Penrith seemed to be pushing through again.

While he himself was quietly guided by the tenets of the Bible, he nevertheless objected strongly to the compulsory attendance at chapel twice a day. He felt resentful of those students who, he knew, did not believe in it, yet went for appearance's sake.

He objected to those who read, or studied, solely for the material rewards of prizes and fellowships. These prizes were offered at Cambridge for academic accomplishments, but students soon became more interested in winning prizes than in learning for learning's sake. William was not interested in the prizes. Life at Hawkshead had not taught him to compete. He wrote of this much later:

> Youth should be awed, possessed as with a sense
> Religious, of what holy joy there is
> In knowledge, if it be sincerely sought
> For its own sake. . . .

He realized quickly that many of the young men at Cambridge were noblemen and gentlemen not intent on serious study. They would someday inherit great wealth and, with it, power. The tutors, or teachers, looked up to them. They were not expected to study and were, in fact, sometimes even put higher on the honor list than they rightly deserved. Some men of noble birth gained degrees without taking examinations. They engaged in much drinking and rioting, wore gowns trimmed with gold or silver lace and caps of velvet with tassels of gold or silver.

William, on the other hand, was a sizar, or scholarship student, and had been a North-countryman with no polish. Socially, this put him just one step above the college servants. His manners, his speech, his dress were different from those of the public school boys. Now, marked by his simple gown as a poor boy, eating leftovers from the fellows' table, living in a dismal apartment over the kitchen, he was no longer the young, promising poet, the "golden boy" he had been at Hawkshead. This proud young man, who as a child had threatened to kill himself rather than suffer the insults of his grandfather's servants, could not accept the indignity of a social slight at Cambridge.

William had come to Cambridge from one of the leading northern schools, and with a year's head start in math over boys from southern schools. He enjoyed reading. He excelled in Roman history, a requirement for freshmen. Yet when he took his examinations in June 1788 at the conclusion of his first year, he did poorly, placing only in the second class. He simply did not sit for the mathematics section. His disillusionment with college life seems to have led to an obstinate refusal to read the required work and, in this way, to reject every real advantage he had in the world. He did, however, read for his own pleasure, no doubt an outgrowth of his inborn desire to have his own way. Dorothy wrote to Jane: "He reads Italian, Spanish, French, Greek, Latin and English, but never opens a mathematical book."

It is highly likely that William spent more time studying than did those students who were pursuing the required course of study. Cambridge University had, in fact, been declining since the beginning of the eighteenth century. Its standard of scholarship had dropped to a low level. Its masters were very young, trained not in the classics but in mathematics. Tutors, one or two per college, depending on the size of the college, did most of the teaching. A man might become a fellow, or senior tutor, at the age of twenty-two to twenty-four, but incomes were so low that many resigned to become clergymen or to enter other professions. It was not until 1850, long after William had graduated, that Cambridge University began to be modernized.

Cambridge, then, did not live up to the very high expectations William had had of university life. But he remained that strange paradox—a rebel and a gentleman at the same time. On the one hand, he was conscious of his duty and responsibility to his family, who expected him to pursue a career in the church or the law. Either of these professions were socially acceptable then, and would, he knew, allow him to become economically independent of his family. On the other hand, he wanted desperately to be honest with himself. William always exhibited good manners, had a high regard for family, conformed in dress to the university men of the day (he even powdered his hair), but he could not conform in his ideas. As he himself wrote later, he was "not for that hour or that place."

But he was not altogether unhappy. After his initial disenchantment with Cambridge, he renewed many friendships and resumed his boyish high spirits. Soon he was riding horses through the countryside, sailing boisterously on the River Cam, and attending after-dinner wine parties. Once, while attending a party in what had been Milton's rooms in Christ's College, he drank so much that he became quite drunk and had to run through town in order to avoid being late for chapel. He made excuses to himself by telling himself that he had been toasting Milton, drinking to this great and revered poet. But he never again drank so much. He learned what most college freshmen usually do—that there is a limit to one's capacity for alcohol.

Chapter 7

A Dedicated Spirit

William's first vacation from Cambridge, in the summer of 1788, brought much joy, and it was then that he first defined the purpose of his life. He returned, not to Penrith, but to Ann Tyson's cottage as naturally as to his "home."

He traveled alone from Cambridge by coach north to Kendal, and from there continued on foot. It was six miles to the Windermere ferry, but when this finally came into sight, William forgot how tired he was and "bounded down the hill," shouting to his friend the ferryman on the opposite shore. The old man quickly brought his boat across and extended a hearty welcome to the boy.

After the brief ferry ride, William had another hour's walk. Then, turning a corner, he saw the snow-white church on the hill and finally—Greenend.

As he walked down the path to Greenend, Ann's little red terrier, William's constant companion on his walks in Hawkshead before he left for Cambridge, darted out to greet him. The dog's noisy barking brought Ann to see what was causing the excitement. She was startled to see William standing there, and her eyes filled with tears of pride and joy as she threw out her arms to him. She was delighted to see him, this wild little boy who had grown suddenly into a sophisticated young man with fashionable clothes and powdered hair.

Ann immediately hurried him off to show him to all her friends. William was somewhat embarrassed, but nevertheless happily accompanied her into Hawkshead, delighted just to be home again. When they returned from town, Ann and William walked through the garden of Greenend and saw the spreading pine tree with the broad stone table underneath—"Our summer seat in many a festive hour." Later,

> Delighted did I take my place again
> At our domestic table: and dear friend!
>
> . . .
>
> Can I leave untold
> The joy with which I laid me down at night
> In my accustomed bed.

First, though, as the sun was setting, William set out alone, accompanied as of old by only the little terrier, to walk again in the fresh air of the woods and fields and mountains.

If William had been disconsolate during his year at Cambridge, the summer in his beloved hills filled him with hope for the future. For as the summer wore on, William came to view the people of Hawkshead with a different eye. He now saw the simple woodsman in the woods, the shepherd on the hills, even his old dame nodding over her Bible in a different light. He came to love them even more now that he could compare them to the sophisticated inhabitants of Cambridge.

William had always been an enthusiastic dancer, and one evening early in the summer he decided to attend a country dance with some of his old friends. He discovered there that some of the girls he had known before leaving for Cambridge had also grown up—as suddenly, it seemed to him, as his growing up had seemed to Ann. But beautifully so. He had such a good time that it was not until four o'clock in the morning that he finally started on his two-mile walk home, exhausted but exhilarated.

As the sun came up over the mountains, William beheld a morning more glorious than he had ever seen before:

> The solid Mountains were as bright as clouds;
> Grain-tinctured, drench'd in empyrean light;
> And in the meadows and the lower grounds,
> Was all the sweetness of a common dawn,
> Dews, vapours, and the melody of birds
> And Labourers going forth into the fields.

It was then that the direction his life must take became clear to him:

> My heart was full; I made no vows, but vows
> Were then made for me; bond unknown to me
> Was given, that I should be, else sinning greatly,
> A dedicated Spirit.

While this did not mean he consciously decided, at that time, to become a poet, he did begin composing "An

Evening Walk" then. The poem described vividly the beauty of the Lake District where

> Far from my dearest Friend, 't is mine to rove
> Through bare grey dell, high wood, and pastoral cove;
>
> . . .
>
> Where twilight glens endear my Esthwaite's shore
> And memory of departed pleasures, more.

"An Evening Walk," no doubt written to Dorothy, his dearest friend, was a melancholy description of the landscape of his childhood, remembered with an observant eye, an acute ear, and much love.

It was probably about this time that William, wondering about his future, wrote in his notebook, among some scribbled fragments of poetry and prose, "Shall I ever have a name?"

In the fall William returned to Cambridge, as he knew he must, but withdrew into himself and began to think seriously of writing. It became his habit during the next two years to walk in the college garden after dark, pacing up and down its walks, and compose poetry. This method of writing was to become a lifelong habit, and as he walked and talked, "like a river murmuring to itself," he often provoked speculation that he was "eccentric."

At Cambridge he continued work on "An Evening Walk." William's youthful experiences—both the scenes he had observed and the poets he had read—are evident in "An Evening Walk." He used as models all the landscape poets who had delighted him as a young boy—

Milton, Spenser, Gray, Pope, Beattie. But, he said in his old age, "There is scarcely an image in it which I have not observed."

"An Evening Walk" exhibits the limit of William's imaginative and intellectual faculties before a decisive crisis that was soon to come, but it is the best example of the standards he set for himself and of his early poetical genius.

William was never able to carry a tune, but he did have a finely trained ear for natural sounds, which he used throughout his writing. In "An Evening Walk" the sound of the landscape is beautifully evident in the last lines:

> The song of mountain streams unheard by day,
> Now hardly heard, beguiles my homeward way.
> All air is, as the sleeping water, still,
> List'ning th' aereal music of the hill,
> Broke only by the slow clock tolling deep,
> Or shout that wakes the ferry-man from sleep,
> Soon follow'd by his hollow-parting oar,
> And echo'd hoof approaching the far shore;
> Sound of clos'd gate, across the water borne,
> Hurrying the feeding hare thro' rustling corn;
> The tremulous sob of the complaining owl;
> And at long intervals the mill-dog's howl;
> The distant forge's swinging thump profound;
> Or yell in the deep woods of lonely hound.

Landscape painting was becoming very popular in the eighteenth century, and all through his life William appreciated this type of art. He developed a great respect for the men who painted landscapes and was once moved to praise, in poetry, the

> Art whose subtle power could stay
> Yon cloud, and fix it in that glorious shape

In "An Evening Walk," despite his youth, William was able to achieve a visual effect even beyond painting.

In November 1788, shortly after William's return to Cambridge, Dorothy "escaped" from Penrith, when she accepted an invitation to live with her Uncle William Cookson and his new wife, Dorothy Cowper, at Forncett Rectory, near Norwich—only fifty miles from Cambridge. She paid a brief but happy visit to William and Richard at school on her way.

She wrote to Jane Pollard of this visit:

> The buildings, added to the pleasure of seeing my Brother very well and in excellent spirits, delighted me exceedingly; I could scarcely help imagining myself in a different country when I was walking in the college courts and groves; it looked so odd to see smart powdered heads with black caps like helmets, only that they have a square piece of wood at the top, and gowns, something like those that clergymen wear; but, I assure you (though a description of the dress may sound very strange) it is exceedingly becoming.

Dorothy then continued on to Forncett, where she was soon very happy running a small Sunday school for nine little boys and girls, "one very bright, some very tolerable, and one or two very bad." She taught them to read, spell, and learn by heart "prayers, hymns and catechisms." She was delighted with this and with her freedom and leisure to "read, walk and do what I please."

William visited her there briefly the following June, completing her happiness.

Chapter 8

To Be Young Was Very Heaven!

At the end of his third year at Cambridge, William once again defied tradition. Although he had some pangs of conscience and knew that confronting his family with his decision would be unpleasant, he had a strong desire to make the most of his last summer vacation, and he decided that, instead of studying for his approaching examinations, he would go on a three-month walking tour of France and Switzerland to see the Alps.

He never enjoyed any experience more.

William chose as his walking companion his classmate and closest friend at Cambridge, a young Welshman name Robert Jones, a kindred spirit eager for the same kind of adventure as William. Robert, "fat, roundabout and rosy," had a background similar to William's. He had grown up among the mountains of Wales, had been educated at country grammar schools, and was the son of a country lawyer. One of his greatest delights as a child had been walking in the mountains. He, like William, did not take an honors degree at Cambridge, although he did receive a fellowship.

Their friendship, however, was not one of intellectual

attraction. Rather, it was an attraction of contrast. William was tall, thin, rather awkward; and with a long face and a grave expression, he looked old for his years. He was reserved, seeming almost to be holding his emotions in check. Robert, on the other hand, was cheerful, good-natured, sweet-tempered, and affectionate, an excellent complement to William, who was often irritable when traveling.

As they prepared to leave, William did not tell either his Uncle William or Dorothy of his plans. He knew his uncle would object strongly—probably even forbid the trip. Dorothy confessed later that had she known about it in advance, she would have considered it "mad and impracticable." "Pedestrian tours" of the sort they planned were virtually unknown among "gentlemen" of England then, although young men of means often made the "grand tour," visiting the palaces and museums of France and Italy with a leader, and often bringing back valuable art objects.

The two left London (where they were careful not to contact William's brother Richard for fear of the family finding out) on July 11, with little knowledge of the area they were about to explore and very little money. They walked to Dover and, on July 13, 1790, crossed the English Channel to Calais, France, just as the French were celebrating Louis XVI's oath of allegiance to a new constitution. The Bastille (the Paris prison that was the hateful symbol of feudal tyranny in France) had fallen the previous summer, and the French king had become a constitutional monarch. The news had made little impression on William the year before. As a boy of nineteen, he had

had little interest in politics, but now, like most Englishmen, he and Robert delighted in the Frenchman's newfound liberty. As Englishmen, they were immediately popular with the French people they met. Many were *fédérés,* delegates who had been sent from Marseilles to the Federation Festival, and were returning home triumphantly. William and Robert were caught up in the excitement and happiness of the time ("The whole nation was mad with joy"). They found themselves joining in celebrations in towns they passed on their way south, sometimes staying up all night, eating at communal tables and dancing in the streets: "Round and round the board we danced again."

They were carried away by the abstract ideal of liberty:

> Bliss was it in that dawn to be alive,
> But to be young was very Heaven!

The appearance of the two—the one a short, plump Welshman, the other a tall, gaunt dalesman, each with an oak stick in hand and a bundle tied in a handkerchief on his head, dressed in lightweight coats of the same fabric—provoked many turned heads and much good-natured laughter.

The two traveled south from Calais, walking primarily on the main roads, where they enjoyed the wind rustling through the elm trees. Averaging approximately twenty miles a day, they reached Chalon-sur-Saône, three hundred miles away, two weeks later, on July 27. Here they decided impetuously to join a group of Frenchmen on a boat trip to Lyons, down the Saône. While enjoying the excitement and boisterous high spirits of the Frenchmen, William was also able to see and appreciate the peace and beauty of the shores they passed.

At Lyons they set out again on foot, heading this time for the monastery of La Grande Chartreuse, a remote mountain sanctuary where they rested—in silence—as guests of the monks for two days. William had probably read about Chartreuse in the letters of the poet Thomas Gray, a favorite of his. Gray had visited the monastery about fifty years before, and his description of it no doubt appealed to William. Surely, William must have enjoyed comparing it to the ruins of Furness Abbey.

After leaving Chartreuse, William and Robert continued on to see the glaciers at Chamonix, with their "motionless array of mighty waves" and to see Mont Blanc. Impressed by their first sight of the Swiss chalets, so different from the farmsteads of their own countryside, they enjoyed the domestic happiness of the cottagers and the freedom of the shepherds in their mountain haunts.

Continuing into Switzerland, they walked through the Simplon Pass and saw Lake Como. These sights remained for William the most memorable "spots" of the entire walk. The grandeur and majesty of the pass, contrasted with the serene beauty of the lake, remained engraved upon his memory. "The impressions of three hours of our walk among the Alps will never be effaced," he wrote to Dorothy. He also enjoyed the dark-eyed Italian girls, whose charms did not go unnoticed.

While crossing the Simplon, however, William and Robert experienced a great disappointment. Expecting—and hoping—to climb still higher into the mountains, and closer to the clouds, they learned from a peasant that they need not climb anymore. The rest of the way was entirely downhill. They had, in fact, crossed the Alps without realizing it. They walked on through the Alps, on a "narrow track . . . between gloomy precipices." The weather was wet and stormy, and the "river roared at their feet, a raging torrent."

Once they became separated during a violent thunderstorm and spent the night wandering about, looking for each other. Remembering how his father's death had resulted from his being lost in the mountains of Cold Fell one bitter night, and how his mother had died of pneumonia, William must have been distraught, wondering if he would ever find his way out.

Another time, at Gravedona, they were awakened in the middle of the night by the chiming of clocks. Thinking dawn was near, they went out into the woods to see the lake at sunrise, but it was still only the middle of the night. The woods were large, and soon they were hopelessly lost. Finally, they sat down on a rock and waited for daylight.

They saw many waterfalls on their way back, including the famous Falls of the Rhine at Schaffhausen where "the whole stream falls like liquid emeralds." At Lauterbrunnen, after they crossed the stream, they suddenly realized they had been in danger of drowning as the water dashed over the rocks and almost swept them away. Later, at Basel, they bought a small boat and sailed down the Rhine (another hazardous undertaking) to Cologne. Here they sold the boat, then walked through Belgium to

Calais, and were back in Cambridge by the middle of October.

The two had traveled a total of about 2500 miles, 2000 on foot, and had seen "the ever living universe . . . opening out its glories." William reflected in a letter to Dorothy that "scarce a day of my life will pass in which I shall not derive some happiness from these images." And, indeed, the clear way in which he could recall a landscape was given new impetus on this Alpine tour, and his own faith in his creative ability was strengthened.

Perhaps even more important than this effect on his imagination, the journey evoked in him a real love for the French people and sympathy for the cause of their revolution. This feeling was soon to become even stronger and to affect him profoundly.

A true understanding of what Dorothy meant to him was, perhaps, another outgrowth of this trip. She had been his constant invisible companion. "I have thought of you perpetually, and never have my eyes burst upon a scene of peculiar loveliness but I almost instantly wished that you could be for a moment transported to the place where I stood to enjoy it," he told her. He knew that she would understand and respond to his feelings of joy in the natural wonders he beheld.

In December William traveled to Forncett to be with Dorothy and to celebrate her nineteenth birthday on Christmas Day. He found her happy, and she described him as an affectionate brother. Together they walked in the garden, delighting in each other's company. Here they first conceived the idea of someday owning a "little parsonage," where Dorothy could keep house for William.

He, however, was still undecided about the pursuit of a career and felt that he did not want to enter the church.

William's return to Cambridge after his trip through the Alps had been anticlimactic. He was now eager only to complete his studies and leave the university. He did meet its requirements, and on January 27, 1791, in the age-old tradition of Cambridge University, still practiced today, he walked with his classmates through the series of three gates at Caius College, which portray the path of a student: humility, virtue, and honor. Thus, a student "enters with Humility, passes through with Virtue and goes out the Gate of Honour" to receive his degree at the Senate Building, the Parliament of the College.

Chapter 9

Earth Has Not Anything To Show More Fair

Immediately after graduation, in February of 1791, when William was almost twenty-one years old, in yet another rash defiance of tradition and obstinate refusal to follow any of the practical suggestions made by his family, he decided to fulfill once again his burning desire to travel. Accordingly, he set out alone for London.

When he was older, William often said that had he been born poor, he would have become a peddler, and had he been rich, he would have squandered his fortune by wandering about the world. Being neither, he simply hoped that some lucky accident would allow him the chance to travel. In the meantime, he was determined to do the best he could. So despite his family's laments that he would "turn out badly," this proud and stubborn young man, unconcerned with the comforts of life and ready to reform the world, embarked on a four-month visit to London.

William had paid his first visit to London during the Christmas vacation of 1789. He had made the trip in order to be with his brother John before John sailed for

India on the *Earl of Abergavenny* in January 1790. William had approached London on the top of the Cambridge coach with the same excited anticipation he had had when he approached Cambridge as a new student three years before. He had many glamorous expectations of London, carried over, no doubt, from his romantic childhood dreams of the city. But just as his high expectations of life at Cambridge had been bitterly disappointed, so now London was not the golden city of his dreams.

In contrast to the country life and the sights of nature that he knew, the city streets were crowded

> With vulgar men about me, vulgar forms,
> Of houses, pavements, streets, of men and things.

Even in the very short time he was there, he saw London "with that distinctness which a contrast gives."

The prime purpose of his visit was to be with John. Yet he annoyed his brother in a way that was typical of him. He bought a book of sonnets by William Lisle Bowles, which had just been published, and proceeded to read them as the two were walking across London Bridge.

On his return to London a year later, William saw the city in a different light. As an unsophisticated young man from the country, he was impressed by the "endless stream of men and moving things" and by "the wealth, the bustle and the eagerness" of life in the city of London. For London had become a channel for the trade goods that mercantile Britain bought and sold, for the raw materials she brought in and the manufactured products she sent out as the industry expanded. London was then the political, social, and cultural center of England, and people as well as produce poured into the city.

The River Thames was its chief avenue. Hundreds of red-stockinged watermen sailed their wherries, or small rowboats, up and down its streams, transporting passengers. In addition, there were the daily colored and gilded barges of the rich and of the various livery companies. Under London Bridge were merchant vessels from many countries—France, Holland, Spain—which, in a sense, sectionalized the river into foreign quarters. There were also sections for native coastal vessels that brought goods and commodities to the capital.

There were some long, straight streets and beautiful squares, where the ground on either side was paved, not with gold as many believed, but with flat stones so one could walk without danger of being knocked down by horses and coaches. For the most part, however, the city consisted of a maze of narrow, twisting lanes and smelly alleys where the neglected poor lived in rotting houses. While some streets were cleaner and brighter than they had been fifty years before, the hooves of the horses and the wheels of the carriages still flung much dirt to the left and right as they progressed along the roads. Perhaps this can help us to understand the advantage of a curb, and why it is considered proper today for a man escorting a woman to walk between her and the street.

Not interested in the social life of London, William, alone and quietly happy, wandered these streets, often walking at night and in the bad weather he had always preferred. While he was shocked and revolted by the scenes of vice, by the coarseness and brutality, the chaos and sordidness of life in eighteenth-century London, he also saw and admired the beauty and grandeur of the city. As he walked, he felt the sad isolation of all the people he passed:

> the face of every one
> That passes by me is a mystery.

But he saw also the beauty of the new buildings, designed by Robert Adam and just being built, with their larger, rounded windows and wrought-iron balconies, and he experienced the excitement of Covent Garden with its bustling vegetable market and Drury Lane Theatre.

William particularly loved the theater, his "dear Delight," but he couldn't afford to go often. When he did, he enjoyed the Drury Lane and the Sadler's Wells with its

> singers . . .
> Clowns, conquerors, posture-makers, harlequins.

Drama, even then, was important in London. In fact, advertisements for the many theaters occupied much of the front page of the London *Times*.

He saw the pitiful little chimney sweeps peculiar to England at that time. In the early eighteenth century, as chimneys became narrower and coal replaced wood, little boys were used to clean out the chimneys. They were often paupers, about six years old, sold by their parents for a few guineas—the smaller the child, the higher the price. Sometimes they were kidnapped. Since the child had to go up the chimney to clean it, and the flues were often only about seven inches square, even the tiniest child had to be stripped naked to ascend. It was often months before the sores on their elbows and knees healed. Many became deformed from climbing while their bones were still soft, and others suffocated or were burned to death. Often when the children were too terrified to climb, masters would light straw fires beneath them or stick pins into their feet.

Walking through Charing Cross, then as now the book center of the world, William was excited by the array of books in the old bookstalls, and by the print shops. He loved the opportunity to browse, content just to finger some of the books, perhaps occasionally to buy a new edition.

He enjoyed even the smell of the books, which almost made him forget the smell of the coal smoke. For London was then enveloped in heavy smoke. This came from the centers of manufacturing along the banks of the Thames and from the coal burned in glasshouses, earthenware factories, gunsmiths' shops, and dyers' yards.

William's affection for children and his understanding of the natural love of a parent for his child was pointed up when he saw a laborer sitting on a rock in a small grass-covered plot. The man was holding his baby in his arms to breathe some fresh air—yet, at the same time he was trying to shield the child from the sun and breeze to which William had been accustomed all his life.

> There, in silence, sate
> This One Man, with a sickly babe outstretched
> Upon his knee, whom he had thither brought
> For sunshine, and to breathe the fresher air.
>
> . . .

He held the child, and, bending over it,
As if he were afraid both of the sun
And of the air, which he had come to seek,
Eyed the poor babe with love unutterable.

Observing London from the point of view of a countryman, William pitied the city folk their lack of fresh air
and freedom, and he was offended by the environment to
which children were exposed in the city.

William also spent time in the House of Commons,
and was present at an historic quarrel on May 6, 1791, between Charles James Fox and Edmund Burke, the first a
champion of the French Revolution and always a liberal,
the latter becoming more conservative and opposed to
the revolution as it became more violent. William listened
to other debates in the House, and heard the young Prime
Minster William Pitt (whose father he had heard spoken of
in his childhood days at Cockermouth) speak brilliantly.
This very young man (he had become prime minister at
the age of twenty-four) was to bring to English government a new and valuable quality—that of purity. He had
inherited his father's impeccable honor and irresistible
force of character, and he was to lead England wisely for
about twenty years.

William wandered on the banks of the Thames. He saw
London's spires, domes, and palaces rising gracefully
from the water. He saw Westminster Abbey, where British
monarchs are crowned, St. Paul's Cathedral, which was
designed by Sir Christopher Wren, and the Tower of
London, the oldest monument in the city, its chilling gray
stone walls evoking the history of England.

William's twenty-first birthday passed unnoticed in the obscurity of London. But happily, he stood back and surveyed the city as a young man eager to see new sights, new faces—whose curiosity keeps him constantly on the lookout and whose idealism makes him feel he can and must correct the ills he sees and reform the universe. He was determined to enjoy his newly found independence—"to pitch a vagrant tent among the unfenced regions of society." He felt, he wrote later, like "a newly invested knight," who looked "round him with a beating heart."

On a subsequent trip to London in July 1802, as he crossed Westminster Bridge on the top of a Dover coach early in the morning, he saw the sleeping city in the stillness of the dawn, and was moved to write the very beautiful sonnet:

> Earth has not anything to show more fair:
> Dull would he be of soul who could pass by
> A sight so touching in its majesty:
> This City now doth, like a garment, wear
> The beauty of the morning; silent, bare,
> Ships, towers, domes, theatres, and temples lie
> Open unto the fields, and to the sky;
> All bright and glittering in the smokeless air.
> Never did sun more beautifully steep
> In his first splendor, valley, rock or hill;
> Ne'er saw I, never felt, a calm so deep!
> The river glideth at his own sweet will:
> Dear God! the very houses seem asleep;
> And all that mighty heart is lying still!

Chapter 10

The Bravest Youth of France

Graduation from Cambridge was not to be the end of William's studies, as he had hoped it would. When he returned from his travels, believing he was finally finished with formal education, his Uncle William insisted that he return to Cambridge for a short time to study "oriental languages." This, William knew, meant private instruction in Hebrew and Arabic in anticipation of his becoming a clergyman.

But William remained in Cambridge for only two months, from the end of September until the end of November. Then he managed to convince his uncle that it would be more worthwhile for him to go to France. There he could perfect his knowledge of French in order, ultimately, to obtain a position as a tutor to some rich young Englishman and accompany him on his European travels.

Actually, this was only a pretext. Once again, William was procrastinating, an art of which he seemed to be a master. He was trying desperately to gain time—time to make up his mind about a profession, time to follow his wandering instincts, time to write poetry. He had also been enchanted by his previous visit to France with Robert Jones, and he wanted another opportunity to spend time there among its people.

And so on November 23, 1791, we find him waiting in Brighton for a wind to allow him to sail across to France. William landed at Dieppe on November 28 and by December 5 was in Orléans, where he planned to remain. He hoped that by staying there, rather than in Paris, he would not encounter many Englishmen and would therefore be able to learn French more rapidly.

Since the start of the revolution many of the aristocratic families, unwilling to do without their accustomed luxuries, had left the city. Of the young men who remained, some joined a society called "Friends of the Constitution," and some were beginning to leave to join the revolutionary army. William saw workmen giving up their wages in order to help equip these soldiers to fight on the frontiers, and he watched peasants working in the fields singing in chorus, *"Ça ira."* The enthusiasm of these patriots soon captured his imagination, and he found himself caught up in their cause:

> Meantime day by day, the roads
> Were crowded with the bravest youth of France
>
> . . .
>
> Even by these passing spectacles my heart
> Was oftentimes uplifted, and they seemed
> Arguments sent from Heaven to prove the cause
> Good, pure, which no one could stand up against.

William found rooms at the boardinghouse of M. Gellet-Duvivier, a Royalist and counterrevolutionary, where he had food and lodging for only eighty francs a month. He would have preferred to live at the house of M. André Augustin Dufour, a magistrate's clerk, but it was too expensive for him. Nonetheless he enjoyed the company of the Dufour family, and spent many evenings there. It is highly likely that part of the enjoyment of these evenings was a young woman who was living there at the time—Marie-Anne Vallon.

Annette, as she was called, was warmhearted and affectionate, and was immediately drawn to the tall, blue-eyed young Englishman. That he was four and a half years younger than she, away from friends and family, and in a foreign country whose language he knew but little added to the attraction. Annette was from the town of Blois, where she had been born in 1766, the sixth child of a surgeon and his wife, Jean and Françoise Vallon. Her father, descended from a family of prominent surgeons, had died some years before, and her mother had remarried. Annette, estranged from her mother since her remarriage, had recently come to Orléans to be near her brother Paul, to whom she felt quite close.

Annette was talkative, and her loquaciousness made it easy for William to learn French. He decided not to hire a tutor, and Annette became his teacher. Her freshness, her womanly instincts, her sensitivity made it easy for her to win young William's heart. She quickly melted all his reserve, and soon they found themselves hopelessly, helplessly in love.

William would often steal out of his lodging at night and run through the quiet, starlit streets of Orléans to a secret rendezvous with Annette. They knew there were many obstacles in the way of marriage—he had no job and therefore no visible means of supporting her; he was an English Protestant and she a French Catholic; both families would surely object. But nonetheless they loved each other unreservedly, allowing passion to rule over wisdom, and when Annette left Orléans in the spring of 1792 to return home to Blois, she was pregnant.

William followed her to Blois shortly thereafter, but here it was more difficult for them to be lovers. Blois was a smaller town than Orléans, and Annette was known by many people there. They did manage to wander about Blois a little, and even visited the convent in which Annette had been brought up, but for the most part, they could meet only in secret.

Because of this difficulty in seeing Annette, William sought other companions to occupy his time. It was at this time that he first came to know Captain Michel Beaupuy, who was to become, with William Taylor, his sister Dorothy, and Samuel Taylor Coleridge, one of the four people whom William regarded as having had the greatest influence, for the good, on his life.

Beaupuy was a young French officer of thirty-seven, a nobleman by birth who had abandoned his social position and the esteem of his friends for the cause of the French Revolution. At Blois William boarded in a house with officers of the Bassigny regiment, all, save one, aristocrats. He found that Michel Beaupuy was the only one in favor of the new ideas propounded by the revolutionists. Soon he and Beaupuy found themselves together often, spending time at the patriotic club of Blois, or taking long walks in town, among the neighboring forests, and in places as distant as Chambord and Vendôme.

Until then William had looked at the revolution sympathetically, but "with no intimate concern." What he had read of the revolution had been, for the most part, editorials rather than facts. He had read arguments for and against it, but he had not seen an objective chronicle of the revolution. His ignorance of its actual progress made it difficult for him to comprehend fully the events he witnessed. He had been an observer of events that had failed to move him deeply. He had been a "republican of the head, not the heart."

Michel Beaupuy corrected this. He showed William what a true republican was. One day, as the two friends were walking on a country road, they passed a "hunger-bitten" peasant girl, leading a heifer by a rope. Beaupuy, upset by the sight of such poverty, cried, "Tis against *that* that we are fighting." It was then that William fully understood and became an "active partisan" of the republican cause, passionately concerned with the human catastrophe that was shaking France.

Annette's family, however, seems to have been opposed to the revolution, although at that time Annette herself was still indifferent to it.

As the summer wore on, William became more and more an enthusiastic republican, concerned about the upheaval that was rocking France. His impassioned emotions of love for Annette, anxiety and remorse over the imminent birth of their child, and ardor for the revolution became fused together, and threw him into a state of pathetic confusion. He became more and more Beaupuy's pupil, revering the older man for his beliefs and for the actions these beliefs inspired, for his love of the poor, whom William had learned to admire in the hills of Hawkshead, and for his desire to abolish poverty and bring "better days to all mankind."

Beaupuy was disliked by the other officers, all of whom were of noble rank, for his belief in the necessity of reform and in the sacrifice of their privileges for the welfare of the country. So Beaupuy turned happily to William for friendship. An intelligent and well-read man, he taught William much of the beliefs of philosophers and political writers whom William had never read. Beaupuy loved to lay bare his ideas to his young friend, and William was eager to listen and learn. They became inseparable.

When Beaupuy left Blois with his regiment in July, headed for active service on the Rhine, it was only four months after the two had first met. They never corresponded, and they never met again. But William always treasured the memory of their friendship, and Beaupuy's influence on him never dwindled.

After Michel Beaupuy's departure, William was still prevented from seeing as much of Annette as he would have liked, and he found himself alone much of the time. Now that Annette's condition had become evident, her family was particularly hostile toward him.

It was at this time that he began composing "Descriptive Sketches," his chronicle of his wanderings through the Alps. The poem depicts one of the happiest times of his life; yet it was written while he was in a state of dejection and depression.

Annette was secretly preparing for the arrival of their child. She kept busy by sewing the expected baby's "linen." When she did see William, she asked him to touch and to kiss all these things, particularly a tiny pink bonnet. While this was very much in keeping with Annette's nature, it must have been extremely difficult for the normally reserved young man.

By the beginning of September Annette was forced to return to Orléans to await the birth of her baby. Her condition was now noticeable, and she could not remain in her native town without its becoming common knowledge. So she went to Orléans in the hope that her baby might be born in a quiet place near compassionate friends. William followed her there, but not before he wrote a letter to his brother Richard in London, urgently requesting money.

We don't know whether or not William was allowed to see Annette during this stay in Orléans, but at the end of October he left for Paris, presumably intending to continue on to London. Perhaps he could not bear to allow the sea to separate him from Annette before their baby was born, for despite his statement to Richard that he intended to be in London by the end of October, on December 15, 1792, when his daughter was born, William was still in Paris and received the news there.

The baby was baptized "Anne Caroline Wordswodth [sic], daughter of William Wordswodth, English, and of Marie-Anne Vallon." Annette's brother Paul was godfather, and Mme. Dufour was godmother. M. Dufour represented the baby's father. William Wordsworth admitted that the child was his and gave her his name—at least insofar as the vicar of Orléans was able to spell it.

Chapter 11

I Roamed from Hill to Hill

Shortly after, William returned to London in the hope of obtaining his guardians' consent to a marriage with Annette and part of the money that would one day be his. He no doubt intended to return to France and marry Annette as soon as possible. His inborn caution had precluded his marrying her first and then confronting his guardians with the accomplished fact.

In London his lack of funds forced him to live with his least favorite brother, Richard. Although the two never quarreled, it must have been a rather difficult time for them, for their political views were extremely divergent. They retained a certain closeness despite this, and throughout his life, whenever William needed Richard, his brother never failed him.

William remained in London, rather than return to his native hills, in order to be near people who were aware of what was happening in the world, and where he could read daily news reports of how things stood in France.

> A patriot of the world, how could I glide
> Into communion with her sylvan shades

Erewhile my tuneful haunt? It pleased me more
To abide in the great City.

He remained in London also to publish "An Evening
Walk" and "Descriptive Sketches" in the hope that they
would provide the money he so desperately needed and
fame, which might mellow his uncles—"I thought these
little things might show that I could do something."
Neither the money nor the fame was forthcoming.

Nor was William able to obtain his guardians' consent
to marry Annette. In fact, even his Uncle William, in
the past his only benefactor, when apprised of the situation, withdrew his offer of a title for orders in the
church and forbade William to come to Forncett. The
most devastating effect of this was that he was not able
to see Dorothy either.

Annette, on the other side of the Channel, returned to
Blois with her child. She lived with her family, but in
order to avert a scandal, her family sent little Caroline
to a nurse outside the city. Annette was distraught
at not having either her child or her beloved William
with her. In a letter to Dorothy, with whom she had
developed a friendship through correspondence, she
wrote, "I cannot be happy without [my dear William],
I long for him every day." And in another letter, after
Caroline had been carried past Annette's house without
being taken inside, she wrote, "That scene caused me a
whole day of tears. They are flowing even now."

But Annette's letters were all full of her feelings and
emotions, of her love for William and their child. She
made no accusations, nor did she appear to know or ques-

tion what William was doing. She seems to have had no real understanding of him—least of all to have had any realization that he was a poet.

William seems to have tried to reach Annette in Blois on several occasions but to have been turned back by warnings of danger. For France had declared war on England on February 1, 1793. A journey to France at this time, he knew, would be fraught with difficulty and danger, and while he was stubborn and silently rebellious, his courage was passive rather than active. He would not willingly seek out danger. Something always seemed to keep him from danger, to keep him from going over the cliff.

Still, he was wretched. He was anxious to be with Annette, eager to see his baby daughter, angry at the ministers of his own country, whom he blamed for the war, and longing for the victory of the Republic of France over all her enemies, including England. How upset he must have been when he reflected that his classmates from Hawkshead might be fighting against Michel Beaupuy and his compatriots. How difficult it must have been for him to see England in direct conflict with what he now considered the cause of all mankind.

By the spring of 1793 William was still the wanderer, postponing the choice of a career. He was disgusted with society, powerless to help his loved ones, reluctant to enter a profession, and beginning to hear the insistent call of his genius. He was coming to understand that he must write poetry.

At the same time Annette was being drawn into the conflict in France. She suddenly found herself deeply involved in work to save her favorite brother, Paul, from the Terrorists and the guillotine. Ultimately, she would work in the underground for the Royalists. She would be drawn out of her self-pity by her brother's near tragedy and the violence of the actions around her, and would transfer the passion of her love for William to a passion for the Royalist cause.

While in London William made several unsuccessful attempts to obtain a traveling tutorship. In June, when an old Hawkshead friend, William Calvert, invited William to accompany him on a tour of the west of England, at Calvert's expense, William compromised his pride and accepted. The two headed first for the Isle of Wight, where they stayed for about a month. Then they started west, with the ultimate plan of going into North Wales and then on to Halifax and a secret meeting with Dorothy. It was two years since William and Dorothy had seen each other, for William's prolonged stay in France and then his uncle's forbidding him to come to Forncett had made their meeting impossible. In fact, his Cookson uncles considered him a bad influence and were making every effort to keep him separated from his sister and brothers.

William and Calvert traveled across Salisbury Plain in a light one-horse vehicle called a whiskey. When the whiskey was wrecked in an accident, Calvert rode the horse north, and William walked to North Wales. The three days spent wandering alone on the plain seemed to ease some of the turmoil that had been raging within him, and became the original inspiration for some of his greatest poems, written years later. Walking, once again, seemed to be the means necessary to release his poetic ability.

Homeless and lonely, he continued wandering through Bristol, across the Severn River to the Valley of the Wye River. Here he delighted again in all the sights of nature he had not seen for two years:

> Yet was I often greedy in the chase;
> I roamed from hill to hill, from rock to rock,
> Still craving combinations of new forms,
> New pleasures, wider empire for the sight.

And here he first began to hope that he might someday produce an "enduring and creative" work of poetry about nature.

It was his second visit to the Wye five years later that prompted the beautiful "Lines Composed a Few Miles Above Tintern Abbey." It was here also that he met the little girl who was to become the heroine of "We Are Seven" and the traveling tinker who later became Peter Bell.

From here William walked north to the vale of Clwyd, where his old friend and walking companion, Robert Jones, lived. He arrived there at the end of August 1793 and was happy to remain and relax there for a while with Robert and his family. It was during this time that William wrote "Salisbury Plain," renamed later "Guilt and Sorrow."

Unknown to William, this summer was to be important for another reason. "An Evening Walk" and "Descriptive Sketches," although they had brought their author neither the fame nor the fortune he had hoped for, accomplished an even more significant task. They brought their creator to the attention of a young poet named Samuel Taylor Coleridge and led to the beginning of what was to be one of the most important relationships of William's life. Young Coleridge, then a Cambridge undergraduate, heard the poems read and wrote, years later, "Seldom, if ever, was the emergence of an original poetic genius above the literary horizon more evidently announced." But it was not until several years later that William and Coleridge met.

In the fall William left Wales and spent several weeks in Cumberland, visiting first William Calvert and his younger brother Raisley at Windy Brow, in Keswick, and then his old school friend John Spedding and his family at Armathwaite. He spent the Christmas holidays at Whitehaven with his Uncle Richard's family, as of old. Despite his unwillingness to conform, William was always received warmly by his father's family, and made to feel comfortable in their home. When he left, he promised to return with Dorothy as soon as his Cookson uncles made this possible.

In the meantime his plans for a secret meeting with Dorothy were constantly thwarted. Dorothy was apparently unable to get an escort to accompany her on her journey to Halifax, and young ladies of that day did not travel alone. It was at this time that William wrote in a letter to Dorothy:

> Oh, my dear, dear sister! with what transport shall
> I again meet you! With what rapture shall I again

wear out the day in your sight! I assure you that so
eager is my desire to see you that all obstacles vanish.
I see you in a moment running, or rather flying, to
my arms.

But it was not until February 1794 that the two were
finally reunited at the home of the Rawsons. (They were
their cousin Elizabeth Threlkeld and her husband, with
whom Dorothy had stayed as a little girl.) They remained
there for two months.

In April, despite the objections of their Cookson relatives, William and Dorothy started on what was to be the
first of many journeys together. They went by coach to
Kendal. Then, Dorothy later wrote, "I walked with my
brother at my side from Kendal to Grasmere, eighteen
miles, and afterwards from Grasmere to Keswick, fifteen
miles, through the most delightful country that ever was
seen."

At Keswick they stayed at Windy Brow, which William
Calvert had lent to them. Dorothy enjoyed keeping house
for her brother, and seeing how economically they could
live: "We find our own food, our breakfast and supper
are of milk, and our dinner chiefly of potatoes and we
drink no tea." This was, in fact, an introduction to their
eventual life together at Dove Cottage.

It was at Windy Brow also that Dorothy began the
task she was to continue for the rest of her life—that of
copying her brother's poems. And it was here that she
began her long and arduous task of restoring her brother's peace of mind, happiness, and faith in himself.

They left Windy Brow about the middle of May and

visited relatives in West Cumberland. On their way they passed through Cockermouth and were dismayed to see their old house on High Street deserted and run down. They continued on to Whitehaven, but, while they were there, their Uncle Richard died. In spite of this last sadness, Dorothy never forgot the beauty of the landscape they saw on their journey, nor the joy she derived from viewing it with her brother. Years later she wrote, "I am always glad to see Staveley, the first mountain village that I came to with William, when we first began our pilgrimage together. Here we drank a bason of milk at a publick house, and here I washed my feet in the brook and put on a pair of silk stockings by William's advice."

Chapter 12

She Preserved Me Still a Poet

Near the end of June, William took Dorothy to visit
their cousins, the Barkers, who lived at Rampside, on the
Furness coast, a mile or two inland from Furness Abbey.
He left her there and returned to Windy Brow himself.
He was still homeless, still the wanderer.

When he arrived, he found Raisley Calvert, William
Calvert's younger brother, ill and dying of consumption.
He took it upon himself to nurse the young man, spend-
ing much time and effort caring for him.

Raisley knew he was dying, and was extremely grateful to William. He also felt that William had a poetic
talent that he was not able to utilize because of his anxiety and his poverty. Because of his strong belief in
William, Raisley offered to help him financially and
promised to leave him a legacy of six hundred pounds.
When Raisley died, in January 1795, William found that,
in gratitude, Raisley had left him not the six hundred
pounds he had promised, but the much larger sum of
nine hundred pounds. For the first time since his father's
death, William was financially independent.

Perhaps now, he hoped, he and Dorothy could afford

a home of their own, a home where he could work and where their two younger brothers could visit and feel at home. The five Wordsworth children had not had a reunion for many years. John had been sailing for the East India Company since he was sixteen, and Christopher was in his last year at Cambridge. Both were able to visit Dorothy occasionally, but not as often as they would have liked. William saw them only rarely. It had long been John's sole desire to earn enough money sailing to help William. He wanted to free this brother, whom he adored, from financial worry and thus make it possible for him to write poetry.

When William was sitting at the bedside of the dying Raisley, he had written in a letter to William Mathews, a friend in London, "I begin to wish much to be in Town. Cataracts and Mountains are good occasional society, but they will not do for constant companions." This was an astonishing comment from one who had always derived such joy from nature. It was, no doubt, an indication of the torment raging within him—of his concern about the revolution and his still unfulfilled need for Annette and their little daughter.

Immediately after Calvert's death, William went to London. This time, however, he did not stay with his brother Richard. He stayed, instead, with Basil Montagu, whom he had met while at Cambridge. Montagu was at that time studying law and living in Lincoln's Inn, the law center of London. Their common hatred of the war seems to have been one of the major forces that brought the two young men together.

Montagu, who was the same age as William, was warmhearted and charming, but terribly poor and unhappy. His young wife had died two years before, leaving him with a new baby to care for. Little Basil was now two years old, and Montagu was experiencing great difficulty in raising him.

The two men had become good friends by February 1795. William, trying to encourage and help Montagu, found himself once again in the role of counselor and aide. But as he helped his friend, he also helped himself, for he felt useful and needed and thought of someone other than himself.

It was at this time also that William met and came under the influence of William Godwin, the author of *Political Justice*. Godwin believed in the power of reason and in the doctrine of "necessity." He felt that man was perfectible—only society was faulty. Evil could be overcome if the conditions that produced it were corrected. Godwin's strong faith in man and in the power of reason had a profound influence on William.

William also became friendly with a group of young men—all, like himself, liberals opposed to the war with France, and all Cambridge graduates.

Montagu, in order to support himself and his son while studying law, taught law pupils on his own. One of these, a wealthy young man named John Pinney, was, like Basil Montagu and Raisley Calvert, much impressed by William and eager to do something to help him. Ultimately, it was Pinney who made the realization of William and Dorothy's dream possible—he lent them one of his father's infrequently used houses, Racedown Lodge, in Dorset. It was Racedown that was to become for William truly "a lee-port in a storm," as the senior John Pinney described it.

Racedown was a large, secluded red brick farmhouse in the country. William and Dorothy would be allowed to occupy it rent free on the sole condition that John Pinney and his brother could occasionally spend a few weeks there in order to hunt. The young Pinneys, however, did not tell their father that they had not asked William to pay rent.

Before leaving for Racedown, William was invited by the elder Mr. Pinney to visit him at his home in Bristol. This William did, and it was here that he met the man who was to become so important to him in the next few years—Samuel Taylor Coleridge. William learned from Coleridge that he, too, was an admirer of William Godwin and had been so moved by *Political Justice* that in 1794 he had decided to found a Godwinian state in a remote part of America. Twelve men and twelve women (Godwin objected to the ties of conventional marriage) would hold their property in common, as in the ideal republic described by Plato. This arrangement they would call pantisocracy, which means "all equal government." It might be likened to present-day communal living. But the scheme fell through, and the plan was never implemented. One of Coleridge's partners in the scheme was Robert Southey, a poet and rebel like Coleridge, and William met him at this time too. He also met Joseph Cottle, a bookseller and publisher. William and Coleridge remained in touch from then on. They maintained an active correspondence, sending each other copies of their poems.

At the end of September, when William and Dorothy finally left for Racedown, they took with them little Basil, to be cared for by Dorothy. William hoped the youngster would have a chance to be happy there, and he also wanted to relieve Montagu of some of his responsibility. Montagu was delighted with the plan and offered to pay fifty pounds a year for Basil's care. This he did for two years, but subsequently, for almost a year, the Wordsworths supported Basil themselves.

William also found himself lending part of Raisley Calvert's legacy to Montagu. Montagu, although often borrowing money from friends and pupils and neglecting to repay the loans, did make every effort to repay William on a regular basis, indicating the affection and esteem in which Montagu held William. And, indeed, the two men remained good friends all their lives.

But William appears not to have been very wise in the handling of any money matters. Perhaps this was because he had never had any money before and, therefore, had no experience. Perhaps it was simply his nature. But he seems to have constantly lent money to friends and was often in the position of having to borrow money from Richard.

Friendships, however, were extremely important to William, and he gave his friend sympathy and consideration as well as money. While he was severe in his judgments, he was too sympathetic and close an observer not to see the good in people. And he had a magnetism that drew them to him. All who were near him loved him.

When William and Dorothy were settled at Racedown, they spent their days reading and writing and, when the weather permitted, gardening, riding, hunting, and cleaving wood. Dorothy, delighted to see her brother out of London and back in the country where she felt he belonged, was always ready to accompany him when he wanted to go out. She thrilled to all the sights of nature. Each fresh view, each flower, each bird was a joy to her, to be viewed with a loving and observant eye and to be pointed out to William.

When the weather kept them indoors, William taught his sister Italian and continued his wide reading. They had found the house well stocked with books. In the parlor, their favorite room, two mahogany glass-door bookcases, filled with books, stood in the recesses on either side of the chimney. William read Italian, French, Spanish, Greek and Latin, and, of course, English. He read much poetry, which he loved, and history. His chief reading was English poetry. He knew and enjoyed the minor poets of the eighteenth century, but revered the four great English poets, Chaucer, Shakespeare, Spenser, and Milton, to whom his father had introduced him when he was just a little boy. He wrote later:

> When I began to give myself up to the profession of a poet for life, I was impressed with a conviction, that there were four English poets whom I must have continually before me as examples—Chaucer, Shakespeare, Spenser, Milton. These I must study, and *equal if I could;* and I need not think of the rest.

Dorothy and William led a simple and frugal life at Racedown. The income from the Calvert legacy was slow in coming, and contrary to their expectations, they were still relatively poor. Almost all their meals consisted of vegetables from their garden, and they had no eggs, milk, or meat. But they were indifferent to material comforts and happy just to be together. Perhaps their greatest disappointment was their inability to buy current magazines and newspapers.

William had been unhappy when he first arrived at Racedown. He was still tormented about Annette; he was still unhappy about the war; he was still confused about man and his beliefs; and he had written almost no poetry for the past two years.

Dorothy worked hard to change all this:

> She whispered still that brightness would return;
> She, in the midst of all, preserved me still
> A Poet, made me seek beneath that name,
> And that alone, my office upon earth.

It was she who restored his faith in himself and who provided emotional peace. When Coleridge later added intellectual stimulation, William's recovery became complete.

It was not until October 1796—more than a year after his arrival at Racedown—that William finally felt able to write again. He began "The Borderers," a tragedy in blank verse reminiscent of Shakespeare. Although it was not published until 1842 and has never been produced, it is important because as he wrote it, he was on the brink of recovery. It is often considered his first autobiographical poem and, reliving through it, as he did, his past few years of despondency was valuable therapy for him. Also, it served to "break the ice," and by the spring of 1797 William was composing poetry once again.

The Wordsworths, although happy and content at Racedown now, did, on occasion, find themselves lonely. William, considered eccentric by the poor people of the neighborhood because of his habit of speaking poetry aloud as he walked through the countryside and carrying a small pocket telescope, particularly missed his London friends. So he invited them to come and stay with them. John Pinney came, but William Mathews and Francis Wrangham, an old friend from William's London days, had neither the time nor the money to do so. Mathews, whom William had known at Cambridge, was the son of a London bookseller, and since Wordsworth's return to England had been his most intimate friend and most regular correspondent. Basil Montagu came, but not until the spring of 1797, when little Basil was already past four years old. Montagu was delighted by the transformation in the child.

"Basil," wrote Dorothy, "is my perpetual pleasure. He is quite metamorphosed from a shivering, half-starved plant, to a lusty, blooming fearless boy. He dreads neither cold nor rain. He has played frequently an hour or two without appearing sensible that the rain was pouring down upon him or the wind blowing about him." This was somewhat reminiscent of the young William Wordsworth, playing in the fields near Cockermouth and particularly loving wet, windy weather.

The Pinneys spent much time with them and also kept William in touch with Coleridge. These two had corresponded since their first meeting in Bristol and sent each other copies of their poems, but posting and receiving mail was time consuming, for the Wordsworths had to walk to the post office in Crewkerne, seven miles away.

In addition to the Pinneys and Montagu came Mary Hutchinson, their friend of Penrith days. Dorothy especially welcomed this pleasant companion, and Mary's serene and happy personality no doubt had a beneficial effect on William as well. She stayed all through the spring of 1797, a creative one for William. He had begun to write again and had produced several poems—"Lines Left upon a Seat in a Yew-Tree," "The Ruined Cottage," and "The Old Cumberland Beggar." Mary shared with Dorothy the excitement and work of copying these poems.

It was while Mary was visiting at Racedown, from November until the following June, that Montagu arrived. The four—William, Dorothy, Mary, and Montagu—happily living together and enjoying each other's company, seemed totally unconcerned that they were violating the proprieties of the day.

William and Montagu made a brief visit to Bristol while Mary was at Racedown, and Dorothy, in a letter to Jane Pollard, now married and Jane Marshall, said:

> She [Mary] is one of the best girls in the world, and we are as happy as human beings can be, that is when William is at home; for you cannot imagine how dull we feel, and what a vacuum his loss has occasioned, but this is the first day. Tomorrow shall be better. . . . He is the life of the whole house.

Obviously, William was beginning to recuperate.

On June 6, 1797, the day after Mary left to return home, Samuel Taylor Coleridge arrived. As William and Dorothy watched for him, they saw him leave the high road, "leap over a gate and bound down a pathless field by which he cut off an angle." This meeting of the three, who were to come to mean so much to each other, was perhaps one of the most significant events in their lives.

William and Coleridge immediately began reading aloud each other's works. "The first thing that was read after he came was William's new poem, 'The Ruined Cottage' with which he [Coleridge] was much delighted, and after tea he repeated to us two acts and a half of his tragedy 'Osorio.' The next morning William read his tragedy, 'The Borderers,' " Dorothy wrote to Mary, adding, "You had a great loss in not seeing Coleridge. He is a wonderful man."

Dorothy was immediately attracted to Coleridge, and he to her. He wrote to Joseph Cottle: "William and his exquisite sister are with me. She is a woman indeed! . . . as for that Giant Wordsworth—God love him!"

Dorothy may have had something to do with the intimate friendship that developed between her brother and Coleridge, for there was a very special kind of understanding, a deep spiritual bond between her and this poet. Some of Coleridge's suppressed feelings for Dorothy may have been carried over into an admiration for William.

Coleridge was so happy with the Wordsworths that he remained at Racedown for three weeks, at the end of which time he persuaded them to return home with him, leaving Basil with the ever-present English maid, Peggy. So they proceeded to Nether Stowey, near the north coast of Somerset, where they met Coleridge's wife, Sara, and their baby son, Hartley. Coleridge and William went on foot, Coleridge returning for Dorothy with a friend's "one-horse shay." It was July 2, 1797.

William and Dorothy never returned to Racedown.

Chapter 13

A Precious Gift

William and Coleridge had much in common, although there were many ways in which the two men were different. Both had been born in the country, but Coleridge came from the south of England, whereas William was a North-countryman. Both had been orphaned when young. Both were independent and original thinkers and, therefore, poor. As a result, William was frugal, and Coleridge was always in debt. Their political beliefs were similar—both favored the French Revolution and the cause of the French people. Both had lived in the country most of their lives, and loved the life of the peasants.

While William was outwardly stern and unyielding, hiding the warmth of his feelings under an air of cold reserve, Coleridge was totally unreserved, enthusiastic, and captivating. He became discouraged easily, though, and was not as persistent as William.

Coleridge had been sent to school at Christ's Hospital in London, very different from the country grammar school at Hawkshead. There Coleridge was ill fed and disciplined harshly. Even as an old man, he often dreamed about a brutal beating he had received at Christ's from one of his masters. This was a far cry from the fond memories William had of the gentle William Taylor.

While the two men were both about five feet, ten inches tall, Coleridge was loose-limbed and impetuous in his movements—we remember his leap over the fence to get to the Wordsworths—and William was stately and calm, calling to mind his skillful skating on the frozen lakes at Windermere.

Both had had ill-fated love affairs. Coleridge had had a tender and delicate love for Mary Evans, sister of a former school friend. But he did not marry her. Instead he fell suddenly in love with Sara Fricker, a sister of his friend Southey's fiancée. He fell out of love with her very quickly, but married her anyway under pressure from Southey. The marriage, while it seemed a success at first, was doomed to failure.

William was saved from making the same mistake by the war between France and England. Had he married Annette, as he had so desperately wanted to, he probably would have had to take Holy Orders in order to support her and their daughter, instead of devoting his time to poetry. While Annette might have made a good bishop's wife, she had no intellectual interests and was only half educated. She would have offered her husband little inspiration. Her inability to understand English would have raised an insurmountable barrier—she could never have appreciated the beauty of the verse William was to write. Its rhythm, ideas, sounds would have been lost in translation. Had he married her, William might never have become the great poet he was destined to be. As it was, his affair with Annette was a temporary deterrent to his poetic growth. It had caused him much anxiety, perplexity, and self-reproach.

As William, Coleridge, and Dorothy went to Nether Stowey from Racedown, the Wordsworths must have been struck by the loveliness of the area. Nether Stowey is a tiny country village set in the rolling farms and woodlands of the Quantock Hills. Brooks of clear water flow from the hills to the Severn Sea (the Severn River, which was always referred to by the Wordsworths as "the sea"), across which lies the green of Wales. Coleridge loved the beauty of the Quantock region, and William and Dorothy soon found themselves sharing his enthusiasm.

Coleridge lived in a tiny cottage consisting of two small rooms and a kitchen on the ground floor, and three smaller rooms upstairs. Pretty little Sara struggled to make it a pleasant home for the husband and baby son she loved so much, but the damp walls, dark rooms, and many mice scurrying about, which Coleridge thought it unchivalrous to trap, made this an almost impossible task. The house was barely big enough for the three Coleridges and their maid.

When, in July, they were joined by William and Dorothy and then by the shy and sensitive Charles Lamb, an old schoolmate of Coleridge, it must have been fairly bursting at the seams. The young people (William, twenty-seven, was the oldest) didn't seem to mind, though. They used the house for shelter only, spending most of their time outdoors exploring the countryside.

On one of their rambles William and Dorothy came

upon a large eighteenth-century manor house, somewhat like the old house on High Street in Cockermouth. Set in a park and surrounded by wild woods, it delighted them instantly. The clear pebbly brooks running through the woods were reminiscent of the Lake District. After cautiously exploring the area a bit, they hurried back to Nether Stowey, eager to learn all they could about the house.

Thomas Poole, Coleridge's friend and neighbor, was able to help. Poole, a tanner (one who converts skins into leather) and a farmer, was a leading citizen of Nether Stowey and devoted to many good causes. He supported local schools and hospitals and was active in the English antislavery movement. He was a good and generous man. Coleridge, in fact, rented his cottage in Nether Stowey from Poole. No doubt one of the reasons was its proximity to his friend's house, for Poole had even cut a door in the wall separating the two gardens so that he and Coleridge might go back and forth easily.

Not only could Poole tell the Wordsworths about the house, but he also quickly arranged for them to rent it and the surrounding property—Alfoxden Park. They moved in immediately. It was Sunday, July 16, 1797. They brought Sara and Coleridge with them. Coleridge remained while Sara went home to be with little Hartley. Then she returned for a ten-day visit, no doubt overjoyed to be out of their tiny cottage for a while, leaving Hartley behind with "Nanny." Although they were poor, the Coleridges and the Wordsworths always managed to have a maid. As soon as they were settled, William returned to Racedown for their maid Peggy and little Basil, and their clothes and books.

Alfoxden, with its nine lodging rooms, three parlors, and a hall, was an ideal gathering place for all their friends, and many came. Charles Lamb, who was to become a lifelong friend of William and a respected critic, was the first to come. And Montagu came from London. The Sunday after they arrived, Dorothy and Peggy prepared a huge roast of lamb, sent over by Poole's mother, and entertained fourteen people, including some of Poole's Stowey neighbors, for dinner. The guests were invited to come early so that William might read his tragedy, "The Borderers," under the trees before dinner.

They also entertained the Bristol publisher Joseph Cottle, who often came to hear the two poets read their latest verses, Thomas Wedgwood, the son of the famous potter, William Hazlitt, soon to become one of the greatest writers of English prose, and John Thelwall, a political agitator for parliamentary reform.

Thelwall, who had three years before been tried for, and acquitted of, high treason, arrived at Alfoxden one morning as Coleridge and the Wordsworths were having breakfast. He had walked from London to see Coleridge and, finding Sara alone at Nether Stowey, had brought her along with him to Alfoxden. He remained for a week. His presence in the neighborhood caused much concern among the local inhabitants. In fact, a short time later a spy was sent by the government to check up on the people and the doings at Alfoxden.

An account of one neighbor's suspicions is, to those of

us who know what was really happening at Alfoxden, quite comical:

> . . . The Master of the house has no wife with him, but only a woman who passes for his Sister. The man has Camp Stools which he and his visitors take with them when they go about the country upon their nocturnal or diurnal excursions and have also a Portfolio in which they enter their observations which they have been heard to say were almost finished. They have been heard to say they should be rewarded for them, and were very attentive to the River near them. . . . These people may possibly be under-agents to some principal in Bristol.

Neighbors also noted that the Wordsworths "washed and mended their cloaths all Sunday" and were "frequently out upon the heights most part of the night." Rumor was that they were French spies. This belief was reinforced by the Wordsworths' "foreign" accent. Coming from the North, they spoke with a deep, guttural intonation, a northern burr, quite different from the Somerset accent. Also, the government agent assumed Coleridge's references to "Spy Nosy" referred to himself. Obviously, he had never heard of the philosopher Spinoza, about whom Coleridge was talking.

And, indeed, the Wordsworths were a suspicious-looking pair. William never attended church; he lived a life of seeming poverty and idleness in a large and lonely house; and he wandered among the hills at all hours of the day and night, muttering to himself. Dorothy, wild-eyed and brusque in her manner, was often seen wandering about also. Little Basil, perhaps, caused the greatest speculation. Who was he and where did he come from?

But William and Dorothy ignored these suspicions and the remarks of the inhabitants, and drank in only the beauty and peaceful quality of the area. They were finally completely happy at Alfoxden. William forgot his political passions. He forgot his onetime delight in crowded city life. They ignored the manufacturing centers springing up around them and were grateful to the country for its charms and for the happiness it made available to them. Alfoxden became their home, their playground, a center for poetic creation. And Annette was becoming a shadowy memory.

They enjoyed their friends and their rural life, but were happiest when they were alone with Coleridge. "We are three people, but only one soul," Coleridge wrote of this time. Sara Coleridge was already beginning to fade into the background.

And the year that followed became an *annus mirabilis* for William and Coleridge. They walked, they talked, they dreamed. They inspired one another. They wrote poetry.

Early in the fall, when Coleridge and the Wordsworths were taking a long walk together, Coleridge was suddenly taken ill with dysentery. The frightful stomach pains made it impossible for him to go on, so he stopped for a day at a lonely farmhouse between Porlock and Lynton, while William and Dorothy returned to Alfoxden. In an attempt to alleviate his pain, Coleridge took two grains of opium that he had with him. He fell asleep and dreamed, and saw in his dream the vision that gave rise to one of his most beautiful poems:

> In Xanadu did Kubla Khan
>   A stately pleasure-dome decree:
> Where Alph, the sacred river, ran
> Though caverns measureless to man
>   Down to a sunless sea.

Released from all that had inhibited his previous verse, Coleridge had reached perfection in a trance. Opium, however, was to prove to be his ultimate destruction.

About four o'clock one dark and cloudy November afternoon shortly after this, Dorothy, William, and Coleridge decided on the spur of the moment to leave on another walking tour through the Quantock Hills. As they tramped the first eight miles in the gathering dusk, with nothing more than a razor and toothbrushes in their pockets, William and Coleridge planned "The Rime of the Ancient Mariner," to be written together. By the time it became necessary to seek shelter for the evening, they had planned the narrative outline of the poem and had begun its composition.

Dorothy listened eagerly as Coleridge told William of a dream related to him by Mr. Cruikshank, a Nether Stowey friend. The dream was of a mysteriously navigated skeleton ship. Coleridge then invented the ancient mariner, whom he playfully called the Old Navigator.

William's imaginative mind promptly supplied the story. The Old Navigator would commit a crime, anger his guardian spirits, and cause his subsequent adventures.

William had recently read about the albatrosses often seen near Cape Horn, and suggested that the Old Navigator could kill "one of those birds on entering the South Sea" and then suffer the consequences. So the theme of the poem became the punishment of an insensitive but not an evil man for a thoughtless crime. William also suggested the navigation of the ship by the dead men, but the rest of the story belongs to Coleridge.

The two men quickly realized that they could not, as they had hoped, share the actual composition. The poetry, then, became Coleridge's. William's only two contributions:

> And listens like a three year's child,
> The Mariner hath his will

and

> as long and lank and brown
> As is the ribbed sea sand

are both rooted in his experiences, the first referring no doubt to little Basil Montagu, the second reminiscent of William's childhood visits to the seashore at Whitehaven.

They realized finally that although they could not cooperate on one poem—because their talents and approaches to writing were quite different—they could collaborate on one book, each contributing what he could do best. And out of this came *Lyrical Ballads*.

These two young reformers, both of whom had grown up in a time of revolution, set as their purpose for this collection of poems "awakening the mind's attention from the lethargy of custom." They believed they could shock their readers out of their lack of concern and inactivity. They hoped to awaken men's minds, through their poetry, to promote human well-being. Poetry was their art, but their aims were social and humanistic. They hoped to use their art to educate their readers.

But William didn't begin work on the *Lyrical Ballads* immediately. Instead, he decided to complete his blank-verse poem "The Ruined Cottage." He had written the last forty-five lines of the poem first, at Racedown the year before. He probably composed the story in his head first and then wrote down separate verses as his imagination inspired him.

"The Ruined Cottage" told the story of the Pedlar, a kindly, observant lover of the countryside. As William wrote, the Pedlar became more and more the young Wordsworth himself, experiencing his own love of nature. Eventually "The Ruined Cottage" would become the first book of "The Excursion," and the Pedlar would become the Wanderer.

As we read the poem we can see how William's imagination was beginning to turn back to the scenes of his boyhood—how he was thinking about his experiences as a youth:

> He had received
> A precious gift; for, as he grew in years,
> With these impressions would he still compare
> All his remembrances, thoughts, shapes and forms;

As he worked on this poem, he began to gain self-confidence. He began to feel that the poem might have some value. For the first time he sensed that he had chosen the right profession—that he might someday have a name.

William's mind had arrived at maturity slowly. He had been diverted by Cambridge, by France and all it implied for him, and by Godwinism. But now his imagination was restored, and he was able to dedicate himself completely to poetry. He had made his choice, and he would pursue it.

By March of 1798 he had completed "The Ruined Cottage" and was ready to begin work on the ballads. This spring would be the happiest he had known in many years.

Chapter 14

The Still, Sad Music of Humanity

One warm, sunny day at the beginning of March, a day seemingly heralding the spring that was soon to come, William was sitting outside watching little Basil play beside him. As William enjoyed this first burst of spring warmth and delighted in the happiness and contentment of the child, he wrote quickly:

> It is the first mild day of March.
> Each minute, sweeter than before,
> The redbreast sings from the tall larch
> That stands beside our door.
>
> . . .
>
> Then come, my Sister! come, I pray,
> With speed put on your woodland dress;
> And bring no book; for this one day
> We'll give to idleness.

He then gave the lines he had written to Basil and sent him running to deliver his message to Dorothy.

On another day, pacing in a grove at Alfoxden, he found himself thinking of the little girl he had met five years before at Goodrich Castle, when he had been walking in the Wye Valley. Quickly, he composed the last stanza, starting with the last line, of a hauntingly lovely tale of a child's inability to comprehend the death of her sister and brother, "We Are Seven":

> "But they are dead; those two are dead!
> Their spirits are in Heaven!"
> 'Twas throwing words away; for still
> The little Maid would have her will,
> And said, "Nay, we are seven!"

He went on to complete the poem, except for the first stanza. Finally, unable to write this, he went in to tea with Dorothy and Coleridge, and recited the lines to them. He explained what he had in mind for the first stanza to Coleridge, and said, "I should sit down to our little tea-meal with greater pleasure if my task were finished."

So Coleridge tossed off the first stanza:

> —A simple Child
> That lightly draws its breath,
> And feels its life in every limb,
> What should it know of death?

And the poem was complete.

In three months, from March to May, William composed fourteen poems, including the long "Peter Bell." In all of them the creative joy of that Alfoxden spring is evident.

Lyrical Ballads, when it was published by Joseph Cottle late in 1798, marked a new epoch in the history of English literature. It ushered in the Romantic movement. Its poems, four by Coleridge and fourteen by William, were concerned with the lives and emotions of humble people living in the country. Their style had a simplicity and directness that marked a deliberate break with the artificial diction of the eighteenth century. As such, they appealed to the young, the smart avant-garde, who found in them "the real feelings of human beings, expressed in simple, forcible language." Ballads were originally composed to be heard, not read, and William and Coleridge often chanted theirs together. It might be fun to try to conjure up an image of these two young poets singing their ballads today, while strumming guitars.

But the *annus mirabilis* was coming to a close, and the Wordsworths were soon to be forced to leave Alfoxden. Although the detective who had been sent to observe the Wordsworths at Alfoxden did finally decide that they were not spies, details of their many suspicious actions reached the owner of Alfoxden. She refused to renew their lease, and they were forced to leave at its expiration.

Homeless once again, they decided, with Coleridge, to go to Germany, in order, they told themselves, to learn the language and take advantage of the good market for translations. Accordingly, they wrote to Richard at the end of May requesting money to pay their rent and to pay Peggy's wages before they left. The remainder of Calvert's legacy had not yet been paid. They made arrangements to send little Basil to live with his mother's sister near Huntingdon, since his father could no longer afford to pay for him. Dorothy, distraught at having to give him up, consoled herself by telling herself that it really would not be wise to take him to Germany, and that he now needed the companionship of other children.

On June 10 William went to Bristol, taking with him two more poems for Cottle to include in *Lyrical Ballads*. He returned to Alfoxden the following week, and on Monday, June 25, William and Dorothy left "that dear and beautiful place" forever. They spent a week in Coleridge's cottage, then left for Bristol again, where they stayed with Joseph Cottle for a few days. Both found the city distasteful after their delightful stay in the country.

By July William had developed a sudden longing to see once again the hills and valleys of Wales, where he had wandered alone five years before, so on July 10 he and Dorothy crossed the Severn Sea by the Aust ferry and spent three days walking up the Wye Valley as far as Goodrich Castle, and then back again. As William noted:

> We crossed the Severn Ferry and walked ten miles further to Tintern Abbey, a very beautiful ruin on the Wye. The next morning we walked along the river through Monmouth to Goodrich Castle, there slept, and returned the next day to Tintern, thence to Chepstow, and from Chepstow back again in a boat to Tintern, where we slept, and thence back in a small vessel to Bristol.

On their return William wrote "Lines Composed a Few Miles Above Tintern Abbey."

> No poem of mine was composed under circumstances more pleasant for me to remember than this. I began it upon leaving Tintern, after crossing the Wye, and concluded it just as I was entering Bristol in the evening, after a ramble of four or five days, with my Sister. Not a line of it was altered, and not any part of it written down until I reached Bristol.

There they went directly to Cottle's house on noisy Wine Street, where William set the poem down on paper for the first time, then gave it to the publisher to be included in *Lyrical Ballads*.

"Tintern Abbey," written at the conclusion of an unusually happy year, is William's prayer of thanksgiving for his ability to see, enjoy, and retain a landscape, as well as a description of the changes in his feelings over the past five years:

> . . . I cannot paint
> What then I was. The sounding cataract
> Haunted me like a passion . . .

But now

> . . . That time is past,
> And all its aching joys are now no more,
> And all its dizzy raptures. . . .
>   . . .
> . . . I have learned
> To look on nature, not as in the hour

> Of thoughtless youth; but hearing oftentimes
> The still, sad music of humanity

He had learned that nature and humanity could be combined in his affection.

In "Tintern Abbey" he seems to have felt himself in full control of his talent. He knew where he was going and was confident in his ability. For his year at Alfoxden had restored his self-identity, which had been destroyed by his despair of the years before. Dorothy, all sensibility, had helped him find once again the beauty in nature, and Coleridge had helped him to think again.

It was Coleridge who offered the intellectual stimulation, the praise, and the faith in William that he so desperately needed. William had needed someone to help him emerge from his solitude; he had needed a creative mind to stimulate his own; he had needed the companionship of an admiring, friendly, outgoing young man. All this Coleridge supplied in abundance.

To Dorothy, though, he owed his greatest debt, and "Tintern Abbey" is another tribute to her. For William recognized what she had done for him—what his sister had meant to him in the last few years:

> For thou art with me here upon the banks
> Of this fair river; thou my dearest Friend,
> My dear, dear Friend; and in thy voice I catch
> The language of my former heart, and read
> My former pleasures in the shooting lights
> Of thy wild eyes. Oh! yet a little while
> May I behold in thee what I was once,
> My dear, dear Sister!

He prayed that her untamed, primitive delight in nature, which was the inheritance of her childhood, would remain with her and

> When these wild ecstacies shall be matured
> Into a sober pleasure

her mind might become

> A mansion for all lovely forms

to sustain her in future years.

While their *annus mirabilis,* the year from July 2, 1797, to July 2, 1798, was truly a fruitful and wonderful year for both William and Coleridge, each poet would have been quite different without Dorothy. During the period from January 20 until May 22, Dorothy kept a journal. Her minute observations of all the sights and sounds of their daily walks together, written in poetic prose, were a storehouse of memories for the two poets and became the raw material of their poetry. Much of Coleridge's "Christabel" and "The Rime of the Ancient Mariner" can be recognized there, as well as many actual phrases of some of William's poems.

Dorothy did not think of herself as a writer, but she did have a remarkable talent for writing prose, and she saw with a poet's vision. Her descriptions were, at times, more sensitive even than her brother's. He, in turn, could incorporate her vision and his own into his poetry. He may not have realized then that the material he was borrowing from her and fashioning into new shapes was already gold.

Chapter 15

'Tis Past, That Melancholy Dream!

On September 15, 1798, at eleven o'clock in the morning, Dorothy, William, Coleridge, and a young man named John Chester set sail in the Hamburg packet on its regular run across the North Sea from Yarmouth to Hamburg, Germany. Sara Coleridge remained at home with the children. Coleridge had decided that it would be too expensive to take them and had invited instead his young friend and disciple.

Dorothy soon found that she was not a good sailor. She was ill from Sunday until Tuesday, almost the entire journey, and was forced to remain in her cabin. On Tuesday, when she did go on deck for her first glimpse of Germany, she wondered if the trip had been worth the agony. It's an ugly, black-looking place, she thought. Later, though, sitting on deck in the moonlight with her brother and their two friends, she drank some tea and began to feel a little better.

The next morning they docked at Hamburg. Here they stayed at a small inn called Der Wilde Mann. They found the city dirty and full of filthy smells, a "sad place," where they were cheated and treated rudely. But they met Friedrich Klopstock, considered the "father of German poetry," and had many pleasant conversations with him. Their only other happy times came in Remnant's English bookshop, where they often rested and read, and where they bought Gottfried Bürger's poems (which William Taylor had translated) and Thomas Percy's *Reliques*.

They met with disappointment also. They were not able to learn German, as they had hoped. They had intended to live with a German family, as William had done in Orléans, where conversation with members of the family would enable them to learn the language quickly and easily. But this arrangement was much more expensive in Germany than it had been in France, and they found they couldn't afford it. So they lived by themselves, comfortably and quietly, but with no one to talk to except each other.

Finally, after much consideration, they decided to separate. Since Coleridge was at that time receiving an annual grant from the Wedgwoods, he and John Chester could afford to go to Ratzeburg, a small town nearby, and then on to a university, where they might study German philosophy and science. William and Dorothy decided, quite naturally, to go toward the more picturesque country in the south. Here they hoped to live quietly and cheaply. All felt that by separating they would not be tempted to speak English to one another, and thus might learn German more readily. William and Dorothy hoped to be able ultimately to earn money translating German, for this was a popular and profitable occupation then.

So on October 3 Coleridge left for Ratzeburg, where he found lodging in a pastor's home and did ultimately become as proficient in German as William was in French. Several months later he went on to Göttingen, where he came under the influence of Immanuel Kant.

William and Dorothy went to Goslar, an ancient little town at the foot of the Harz Mountains. On their way to Goslar, at a stopover in Brunswick, William bought apples and bread for a cheap picnic breakfast. Then Dorothy "carried Kubla to a fountain in a neighboring market-place," where she "drank some excellent water." Obviously, Coleridge was always in their thoughts. The drinking can they used on their journeys was playfully nicknamed after Coleridge's builder of the pleasure dome. They never lost their sense of humor.

William and Dorothy had chosen Goslar simply because the local coach happened to be going there. They found very soon that they should have been more careful in their selection. The coldest weather of the century hit Goslar that winter, and Dorothy and William were forced to remain indoors for the better part of five months. When they were able to venture out, they were ignored by the local inhabitants, who looked on them with suspicion. In Germany "sister" was the accepted polite term for "mistress."

There was no library in Goslar and therefore no books to read. They read only the few that they had brought with them. "As I had no books I have been obliged to write in self-defense," William wrote to Coleridge. When he was not reading, he was "consumed by thinking and feeling." And these feelings began to force themselves into poetry.

At the same time, though, he was troubled by a terrible pain in his side, which seemed to bother him whenever he wrote. Dorothy, watching him, remembered that she had noticed this many years ago, when he was still a schoolboy, and her heart went out to him. This pain was to remain with him whenever he worked, and persisted throughout his life. It reached its peak in Goslar—as did his poetry.

The absence of Coleridge, the isolation of daily life in this freezing mountain village, the lack of books, the presence of his sister with all the memories of childhood that her presence evoked—these combined to make his mind reflect back on his own experiences. And so began one of his most productive periods of writing and his greatest work—the poem of his own life, "The Prelude." For as he recalled his childhood days in the Lake District, he turned his memories into verse.

In addition to the first book of "The Prelude," including the well-known descriptive passages about nutting and skating, he also wrote the famous Lucy poems, among them his beautiful tributes to Dorothy. (The Lucy in most of these poems is most likely Dorothy, the name Lucy being used for its rhythm.)

Written two years later, but certainly an outgrowth of the homesickness that was gripping him then, the last of his Lucy poems reflects his final rejection of all that was foreign to England, and possibly even of Annette:

> I travelled among unknown men,
>   In lands beyond the sea;
> Nor, England! did I know till then
>   What love I bore to thee.
>
> 'Tis past, that melancholy dream!
>   Nor will I quit thy shore
> A second time; for still I seem
>   To love thee more and more.

As he wrote, William sent his poetry off to Coleridge for approval and criticism. Even though they were apart, he still needed the encouragement of his friend.

In the spring, when they were finally able to travel again, William and Dorothy set out for Hamburg and the packet back to England. On their way they stopped briefly in Göttingen to see Coleridge. Dorothy begged him to come to the north of England with them, where they could "explore together every nook of that romantic country, and I would follow at your heels and hear your dear voices again."

William was eager to return to his beloved North country, and to be near a great library, but Coleridge felt that he must live near his old friend Thomas Poole, and so expected to return to Nether Stowey. They parted depressed and unhappy.

Chapter 16

Here Must Be His Home

When they landed in England in May, William and Dorothy went directly to Sockburn, in Durham, Yorkshire, to visit Mary Hutchinson. Here, the unmarried Hutchinson sisters kept house for their unmarried farmer brothers, as was the custom then. Their house, on the banks of the Tees River, had been built by their uncle and then left to them when he died. Dorothy, describing it to a friend, called it

> an excellent house, not at all like a farm-house. They seem to have none of the trouble which I used to think must make farmers always in a bustle, for they have very little corn and only two cows. It is a grazing estate, and most delightfully pleasant, washed nearly round by the Tees (a noble river) and stocked with sheep and lambs which look very pretty, and to me give it a very interesting appearance.

Here William could renew his friendship with Mary Hutchinson. He felt comfortable and at ease with her, and very happy with this family. He was probably not yet in love with her, but found a sense of peace here and was able to continue writing poetry.

He composed the second book of "The Prelude," writing about his boyhood rides to Furness Abbey, boating on Lake Windermere, and his wait for the ponies at Hawkshead. He was trying now, as he reflected on the emotions of his boyhood, to draw some conclusions on the nature of man.

But he was still troubled by the recurring pain in his side and by the problem of money. His old friend Montagu was now working hard at the practice of law, but was still so poor he was unable to repay a loan that Richard Wordsworth had made to him, and Richard was threatening to send him to "gaol" for nonpayment. William himself was desperate for money and unable to help Montagu. Fortunately, John Pinney and Josiah Wedgwood both came to their aid financially.

But William missed Coleridge. Just as his poverty kept him from making the trip south to Nether Stowey, so Coleridge's lack of funds made it impossible for him to travel north. Finally, Cottle, worried about William's health and seeing how desperately Coleridge wanted to visit his friend, decided to go to Sockburn, taking Coleridge with him as his guest. So, on October 22, traveling luxuriously in a post-chaise, the two set off for the four-day journey to Yorkshire.

When they arrived on October 26, 1799, all were overjoyed to see one another. Perhaps by the time Coleridge arrived, William and Mary were already beginning to fall in love, for Coleridge immediately embraced Mary as a sister. Within a short time he too found himself in a similar position. He suddenly realized that he was finding in Sara Hutchinson an understanding that he could not have from his own Sara. And here began the great, but unfulfilled, love of his life.

On the day after he arrived, Coleridge set out with William to see the Lake Country. Cottle, his mission accomplished, returned home. Two days later they were unexpectedly joined by William's brother John, who was on leave between two voyages of the East India Company. He had come north to attend the funeral of their Uncle Kit Cookson, who had died suddenly at Newbiggin Hall. Christopher Crackanthorpe Cookson had left his niece Dorothy a hundred pounds, but no one else was named in the will. William did not visit his aunt to pay his respects. He had not forgotten his treatment at the hands of his uncle when he was a boy.

But he was overjoyed to see John, whom he had hardly seen since John had left school to go to sea. Coleridge, too, immediately liked the shy young sailor "with a swift instinct for truth and beauty."

The three set off together now, heading for Hawkshead and all of William's schoolboy haunts. Here William proudly showed Coleridge all the sights that had delighted him, much as a New Yorker might show off the Empire State Building and the glories of the city to an out-of-towner. On their way they visited the Reverend Thomas Myers, the widowed husband of William's aunt, Ann Wordsworth, and father of John Myers, who had accompanied William to Cambridge. They visited John Fleming's family at Rayrigg on Lake Windermere and then went on to Hawkshead, where they learned that Ann

Tyson had died three years before at the age of eighty-three.

They stayed in Hawkshead only one night, then continued on to Rydal and Grasmere. William had seen Grasmere once when he was just a boy, rambling from Hawkshead over the Langdale Pass, and had been enchanted with it. He wrote of his memory of it: "What happy fortune were it here to live." Living there had been a recurring adolescent dream of his:

> Here must be his home
> This Valley be his world.

Now, excited again at the prospect of living in the North, which was his true love, and of living here in Grasmere, he wrote to Dorothy with that suppressed excitement so characteristic of him, "There is a small house at Grasmere empty which we might take, but of this we will speak."

No doubt he was encouraged in this venture by John, who offered him the money to accomplish it. It was still John's fervent wish that his sister and brothers should have a home of their own.

They continued their trek together until John had to leave to return to Newbiggin and Coleridge headed back to Sockburn. Coleridge was returning to bid good-bye to Dorothy and to Sara Hutchinson, and would then go on to London, where he had been offered a position writing political and literary articles for the newspaper *The Morning Post*. William remained a little longer, returning to Sockburn on November 26, one month after he had left.

Chapter 17

With a Passionate Welcoming

Three weeks later, on December 17, after much consultation, William and Dorothy set out for Grasmere, a journey of eighty miles. They made the first part of the trip on horseback, Dorothy riding pillion with George Hutchinson, from whom they had borrowed the horses and who was accompanying them partway. When George returned to Sockburn with the horses, William and Dorothy continued on foot, often in freezing weather and blinding snowstorms. But they were unconcerned. They were happy and excited at the prospect of soon realizing their long-awaited dream of a home of their own.

After three days of walking, weary but eager to be in Grasmere, they arrived at Kendal, where they bought some furniture and then rode with it in a post-chaise to Grasmere. They arrived at the house at dusk on December 21, 1799, the shortest day of the year.

> When this Vale
> We entered, bright and solemn was the sky
> That faced us with a passionate welcoming,
> And led us to our threshold. Daylight failed

Insensibly, and round us gently fell
Composing darkness, with a quiet load
Of full contentment.

They were home.

The cottage was dark; the beds were unmade; and only a handful of reddish cinders glowed in the fireplace. But they were young; they were happy; they had achieved their goal. Old Molly Fisher, who had been asked to light the fires in the house before their arrival, loved to recall Dorothy's appearance: "I mun never forget 't laal [little] striped frock and 't laal straw bonnet as ye stood here."

The house, formerly an inn called The Dove and Olive Bough, and today known as Dove Cottage, had no name then. The Wordsworths' address was simply "Town End, Grasmere." The house had latticed windows and a wainscoted ground-floor room, which Dorothy used as the kitchen. The other downstairs room became her bedroom. Upstairs, one room became the living room; one was William's bedroom; and two tiny ones remained empty, to be used as guest rooms. One of these was "unceiled," and Dorothy papered it with newspapers.

From their windows they could see across the fields to Grasmere Lake and Silver-How and Easedale fells. From their door a natural path led down to the lake. Behind the house was a "little nook of mountain ground," which rose steeply and contained some fruit trees. In fact, it rose so steeply that William and Dorothy eventually cut a doorway out onto it from the staircase landing. They called this area "the orchard" and spent many hours here, enjoying the magnificent view, thinking, talking, writing.

Dorothy and William found much happiness here. Together they worked in the garden as soon as the ground thawed: "My trees they are, my sister's flowers." They built a wall of stones, enclosing their house and garden from the road, cleared the rocks and the little well, and planted the flowers they found on their walks or received as gifts from the neighbors. William and their neighbor John Fisher, Molly's brother, laid stepping-stones in the grass to the terrace.

Their first year passed as probably their busiest and happiest one. They planted peas and trained runner beans up the house on strings. They went fishing and caught trout and pike for dinner. And right from the beginning the tiny cottage was full to overflowing with visitors.

William and Dorothy were happiest when John came for a long visit while waiting to take command of the *Earl of Abergavenny,* the ship of which he had just been appointed captain. John stayed from January until September, and the close relationship that had existed among the three when they were very young was finally reestablished.

John shared all their likes and their habits. William called him "a poet in everything but words." He was silently enthusiastic, loving all quiet things, particularly the night. The stars and the moon were his chief delight. His father had called him "Ibex, the shyest of all the beasts."

John loved the cottage as William and Dorothy did and loved particularly a grove of Scotch firs, "thickly planted," just off the road to Ambleside, near the shore of Rydal Water. Here he often paced back and forth and ultimately wore a path through the trees. William and Dorothy called this "John's Grove."

He fished with them (once he returned from the lake with a pike weighing seven and a half pounds), and he walked with them. Their longest walk occurred when William and John set off one day, "cold pork in their pockets," to walk through the Yorkshire dales to visit the Hutchinsons. They were gone for three weeks. It was at this time that Dorothy began her Grasmere journal, written partly to ease her loneliness, but mostly "because I shall give William pleasure by it." She recorded here all the details of their daily life, giving us a view of her boundless, childlike delight in nature, which William treasured so much.

Shortly after William and John returned from Sockburn, Mary Hutchinson returned their visit. She stayed with the Wordsworths for six weeks, from the end of February until early April. She and John spent much time together. They took long walks and became close friends. At this time there was still no talk of William and Mary's marriage, and John became "exceedingly attached" to Mary. The depth of his feelings for her were probably not apparent to anyone until late in 1802, when William and Mary's marriage was imminent, and John wrote to her:

I have been reading your letter over and over again, my dearest Mary, till tears have come into my eyes, and I know not how to express myself—Thou art a kind and dear creature. But whatever fate befal [sic]

me I shall love thee to the last, and bear thy memory
with me to the grave.

The Wordsworths and Coleridge, however, seemed to
think that John would ultimately marry Sara Hutchinson. For John had hoped that, once he had earned enough
money sailing to the East to adequately support his brother
and sister, he would build a house for himself in Grasmere, in a field near their cottage. The family thought
he would then bring Sara Hutchinson here as his bride.

Coleridge, too, hoped for this. He knew, much as he
loved this Sara, that he could never marry her, and that
she, by marrying John, would be no further lost to him
than if she were to remain single.

This would never come to pass, though. By September
29, 1800, the *Earl of Abergavenny* had returned and was
ready to set sail again, with John as her captain. William
and Dorothy walked with him to the top of the Grisdale
Pass, past the tarn where he and William had so often
fished, until they were in sight of Ullswater. From there
John went on alone, running down the rocky mountain,
cheerful and eager to be at sea once again. William and
Dorothy waited and waved until he was out of sight.

It was to be their last long visit with him, for in February 1805 they would receive the shattering news that
John had drowned when his ship was wrecked in Wey-
mouth Bay. The Wordsworths were devastated. A newspaper account of the incident stated that "as the *Abergavenny* was laden with an immense quantity of porcelain
ware and 27,000 ounces of silver, she sank with unusual
speed." John went down with his ship.

This was the greatest shock the Wordsworths were ever to experience. They would look to one another for comfort and consolation, and it was to Richard that William would voice his heartbroken plea: "God keep the rest of us together! The set is now broken."

At Town End, though, in that first year of the nineteenth century, the Wordsworths were still happy. They delighted in their many neighbors, most of whom were the simple farmers William had learned to love as he was growing up among them in Hawkshead.

The shadow of poverty hung over many of the farmers, though. Spinning and weaving in the cottages had been steadily declining because of the growth of manufacturing towns nearby. Dorothy wrote in her journal:

> John Fisher talked much about the alteration of the times, and observed that in a short time there would be only two ranks of people, the very rich and the very poor, "for those who have small estates," says he, "are forced to sell, and all the land goes into one hand."

The Wordsworths continued to enjoy their many visitors. Coleridge came in April of 1800, and then again at the end of June with Sara and Hartley, when they stayed a month. He then moved his family to Greta Hall, a spacious two-family house in Keswick, thirteen miles away. Coleridge, unable any longer to resist the magnetism of William, had decided that since William obviously was not about to move south to be near him, he must move north. Then started once again the constant communion between the two families—a sort of "shuttle" between Town End and Greta Hall reminiscent of the days at Alfoxden and Nether Stowey.

Once again the lives of the three families—the Wordsworths, the Coleridges, the Hutchinsons—were intertwined. All were dependent on one another. All, that is, save Sara Coleridge, who, in her strong conventionality, was unable to join in their nocturnal walks and was intolerant of their lack of concern for clothes, for time, for appearances. She considered William and Dorothy wild. And she was unhappy in this part of England. She would have much preferred staying in Nether Stowey, where she had her own friends.

A rock on the road to Keswick, called by the group "Sara's Rock," bears testimony to their interlocking friendships. As they made their many treks back and forth to each other's houses, Coleridge, the Wordsworths, and the Hutchinson sisters carved their initials in this rock with Coleridge's penknife:

WW, MH, DW, STC, JW, SH

Sara Coleridge's initials are conspicuous by their absence.

This summer brought still another joy—the unexpected success of *Lyrical Ballads*. All the copies were sold, and William and Coleridge were asked to prepare a second volume. This they did eagerly, adding all the short poems William had written in Germany and since his return. These included the "Lucy" poems, "Joanna" and "Nutting," "Michael," which had been extremely difficult for William to write, and "The Brothers," almost prophetic in its theme and certainly written with his own shy young brother in mind. Coleridge's "The Rime of the Ancient

Mariner" was moved from the front of the book to the end.

This edition included also William's often-quoted "Preface," in which he defined poetry and described his own aims in writing it. "All good poetry is the spontaneous overflow of powerful feelings," he wrote. It "takes its origins from emotion recollected in tranquility."

What William was trying to do in his own poetry was to communicate emotions to his readers by using "language really used by men" and colored by imagination, to make his readers feel the wonder and beauty of ordinary life. This language must be real, it must be pure, it must be universally understandable, even for centuries to come. And this he did. For it was he who reversed the trend of the eighteenth century from attention to towns, manners, and politics to the country, nature, and the inner moral life of man.

William believed in the equality of all human beings, and his poetry reflects this. He felt he could learn something from all—from the Cumberland beggar, the peddler, the discharged soldier, the female vagrant, the leech gatherer.

He, who had spent half his childhood running wild among the mountains, felt also that children should be free, and he objected to what was happening to them as a result of the Industrial Revolution. He saw mothers and fathers being separated and sent to workhouses and their children being sold and "apprenticed" in mills. He feared for the breakdown of the bonds of domestic feeling among the poor and wrote about it in "Michael" and "The Brothers."

The affair with Sir James Lowther, the long and unsuccessful attempts to obtain their rightful inheritance, had cast a shadow of uncertainty over the lives of all the Wordsworth children. They all yearned for independence, and William particularly felt it an "essential part of human dignity." He never complained about his lack of financial independence, nor of the humilities he had endured in his grandfather's house and again at Cambridge, but he was acutely aware of the situation. Perhaps this is another reason he admired the independence of the small farmers in the Lake District, and why they play such a large role in his poetry.

Chapter 18

The Glory and the Freshness
of a Dream

The year 1801 passed quietly and uneventfully. William rested and relaxed. He wrote very little poetry. Catherine and Thomas Clarkson became the Wordsworths' closest friends in the Grasmere area. The Clarksons lived in a house at the foot of Ullswater, which Thomas Clarkson had built, and which they called Eusemere. The two families visited back and forth.

Many of William's old friends came to visit also, among them his London friends and John Marshall, husband of Dorothy's old friend Jane Pollard. The Wordsworths never allowed their writing or reading to interfere with the entertainment of their many friends.

The walks between Town End and Greta Hall continued. The talk about poetry continued, and many nights William, Dorothy, and Coleridge sat up together or walked in the moonlight until the early hours of the morning.

In September William made his first trip to Scotland.

He went to attend the wedding of Basil Montagu, who was now becoming a successful lawyer and was about to marry Laura Rush, the lovely young daughter of a wealthy Suffolk landowner.

In November Mary Hutchinson came to visit again. When she arrived, she, William, and Dorothy walked to Greta Hall to say good-bye to Coleridge, who dared not risk another northern winter and was about to leave for London. Coleridge had recently been plagued by rheumatism, which was aggravated by the dampness of the Lake District. He was ill; his marriage was disintegrating; he was depressed; and he was beginning to take opium regularly.

The four enjoyed a quiet evening at Coleridge's home (Sara had already left for London), but after Coleridge departed the next day, and William, Dorothy, and Mary were headed back to Grasmere, Dorothy broke down. Thinking no doubt of Coleridge's unhappiness, of his illness, of the long absence she felt certain would ensue, Dorothy could contain herself no longer—"At last I eased my heart by weeping." William, trying hard to hide his own grief, for her sake and for Mary's, chastised her for her "nervous blubbering."

The next day, however, secure once again at Town End, Dorothy baked bread and pie, straightened the bookshelves, and mended stockings. The evening found the three of them sitting around the fire, William reading by candlelight, Mary writing to her sister Sara, and Dorothy writing in her journal.

William and Mary found themselves growing closer together now, and by the end of the year they decided to marry. But William had much to do first. He had much poetry to write and he had resolved to see Annette and Caroline.

Soon after this decision, in the spring of 1802, William had a surge of creative power never again equaled. He wrote poem after poem—over thirty in ten weeks—all reflecting his ability to recall the simple thoughts and emotions of his childhood and to translate these into exquisite poetry.

It was at this time that he wrote "To a Butterfly," recollecting his delight in chasing butterflies with his sister in the garden at Cockermouth twenty-five years before. "The Rainbow," celebrating that incredible rainbow he had seen when he was a schoolboy wandering in the hills of Coniston, was written then also. And on the same day that he wrote "The Rainbow," he wrote the lovely "To the Cuckoo":

. . .

> Thrice welcome, darling of the Spring!
> Even yet thou art to me
> No bird, but an invisible thing,
> A voice, a mystery;
>
> The same whom in my schoolboy days
> I listened to; that cry
> Which made me look a thousand ways,
> In bush, and tree, and sky.
>
> To seek thee did I often rove
> Through woods and on the green;

And thou wert still a hope, a love;
Still longed for, never seen.

And I can listen to thee yet;
Can lie upon the plain
And listen, till I do beget
That golden time again.

. . .

The next day, at breakfast, William began his great "Ode on Intimations of Immortality," in which he pondered the glory that had transfigured everything for him in boyhood:

There was a time when meadow, grove, and stream,
The earth, and every common sight
    To me did seem
Apparelled in celestial light,
The glory and the freshness of a dream.

On Sunday, March 28, with the ode only partially written, William and Dorothy left Town End to visit Coleridge, who had returned to Keswick from London. While they were there, Coleridge wrote a letter in verse to Sara Hutchinson which, with the name Sara changed to Edmund, was published several months later as "Dejection: an Ode."

A few days later, on his thirty-second birthday, William left to visit Mary, and Dorothy went to stay with the Clarksons at Eusemere. When William arrived at Bishop Middleham, near Bishop Auckland, where Mary was now staying with Sara and George, he and Mary became formally engaged. They made plans for a simple autumn wedding. They would be married in Brompton Church, near Tom Hutchinson's new home, Gallow Hill, and would then live at Town End in Grasmere. Dorothy would live with them. But first, William told Mary, he must visit Annette and Caroline in France that summer. The past had to be faced. It was a brave decision.

The trip home from Mary's was a difficult one, beset by several problems. First, William lost his way in a snow and sleet storm. Later, his horse fell, and he discovered that it needed new shoes. He was, therefore, compelled to ride very slowly. He began to think back, and his mind focused on an incident that had occurred seven years before—an incident concerning his sister and a little glow-worm. And so he composed "The Glow-worm":

> Among all lovely things my Love had been;
> Had noted well the stars, all flowers that grew
> About her home; but she had never seen
> A Glow-worm, never one, and this I knew.
>
> While riding near her home one stormy night
> A single Glow-worm did I chance to espy:
> I gave a fervent welcome to the sight,
> And from my Horse I leapt: great joy had I.
>
> Upon a leaf the Glow-worm did I lay,
> To bear it with me though the stormy night:
> And as before it shone without dismay;
> Albeit putting forth a fainter light.
>
> When to the Dwelling of my Love I came,
> I went to the Orchard quietly;
> And left the Glow-worm, blessing it by name,
> Laid safely by itself, beneath a Tree.

The whole next day I hoped, and hoped with fear;
At night the Glow-worm shone beneath the Tree;
I led my Lucy to the spot, "Look here!"
Oh! joy it was for her, and joy for me!

Even then, immediately after completing plans for his
wedding to Mary, William's thoughts were on Dorothy.
He was particularly anxious to reassure her that his
marriage would change nothing between brother and
sister.

He delighted Dorothy with the poem when he arrived
at the Clarksons'. They remained there another day, then
started home together. It was a windy day, and as they
walked through Gowbarrow Park along the shore of Ullswater, they saw

> a few daffodils close to the water-side. . . . But as we
> went along there were more and yet more; and at
> last, under the boughs of the trees, we saw that there
> was a long belt of them along the shore, about the
> breadth of a country turnpike road. I never saw daf-
> fodils so beautiful. They grew among the mossy stones
> about and about them; some rested their heads upon
> these stones as on a pillow for weariness; and the rest
> tossed and reeled and danced, and seemed as if they
> verily laughed with the wind, that blew upon them
> over the lake; they looked so gay, ever glancing, ever
> changing. This wind blew directly over the lake to
> them. There was here and there a little knot, and a
> few stragglers a few yards higher up; but they were
> so few as not to disturb the simplicity, unity, and
> life of that one busy highway.

None of Dorothy's recordings of the sights and sounds of nature surpasses this touch of creative magic, which she wrote in her journal on April 15. And from this, two years later, came

> I wandered lonely as a cloud
> That floats on high o'er vales and hills,
> When all at once I saw a crowd,
> A host, of golden daffodils;
> Beside the lake, beneath the trees,
> Fluttering and dancing in the breeze.

William went on to compose many more beautiful poems that spring. None of them concerns the woman he was about to marry.

Chapter 19

Dear Child! Dear Girl!

Dorothy, at this time, was concerned about placing any extra financial burden on William once he married, and so wrote to Richard requesting that he make her an annual allowance of twenty pounds. She was already receiving twenty pounds each from John and Christopher, and she felt that sixty pounds a year would adequately satisfy all her needs. She might even be able to "buy a few books, take a journey now and then." This Richard would have done gladly, but in May it became unnecessary. Sir James Lowther, Earl of Lonsdale, died and his heir agreed to pay the twenty-year-old debt owed to John Wordsworth's children, approximately eight thousand pounds, including interest.

In July William and Dorothy finally set out for Calais and the long-awaited reunion with Annette. They stopped first at Keswick to see Coleridge, then went on to Eusemere and a visit with the Clarksons, and finally journeyed to Gallow Hill for a brief visit with Mary. From there they took a post-chaise to London. It was their drive on the Dover coach across Westminster Bridge early on the morning of July 31 that inspired the beautiful sonnet

"Earth Has Not Anything to Show More Fair." On August 1 they were in Calais.

They stayed at an inn in a dirty and smelly neighborhood, in a room next door to one occupied by Annette and Caroline. It was very hot and there was nothing to do there but walk on the beach and, occasionally, swim in the ocean, but they remained for four weeks. Here William, still a young man and in love with Mary, looked at Annette, now thirty-six years old and aged by the anxieties of the war and of raising their child alone, and he realized that a union with her would never work. Ten years had pointed up the differences in their natures, had made him see the impossibility of the situation.

And so William and Annette remained friends, but never became husband and wife. She returned to her native Blois with Caroline, and William and Dorothy returned to London. They were to see each other only once more—eighteen years later.

Now, as before, the eager and generous woman who had captured the young poet's heart ten years before asked nothing for herself. She had brought up their daughter alone; she had risked her life as a monarchist; but she had no accusations, no recriminations. She wanted only to retain the friendship of the now matured man. This she did.

William, no doubt torn by his desire to assist Annette in her dangerous and difficult life and to have his little girl with him, and by his inability to accomplish this, was extremely unhappy. He did, however, enjoy the beautiful evenings:

Dear Child! Dear Girl!

> It is a beauteous evening, calm and free,
> The holy time is quiet as a Nun
> Breathless with adoration;

And he delighted in his lovely little daughter. He may have been disappointed that she was not in some way like himself or like Dorothy, that she seemed not to have their delight in nature, their poetic spirit, but he enjoyed her thoroughly and loved her very much:

> Dear Child! dear Girl! that walkest with me here,
> If thou appear untouched by solemn thought
> Thy nature is not therefore less divine.

Chapter 20

To Tread the Grass of England
Once Again

"Here, on our native soil we breathe once more." Thus
William and Dorothy returned to England at six o'clock
on the evening of August 29, disenchanted with what they
had seen in France, relieved and happy to be home again:

> Thou art free
> My Country! and 'tis joy enough and pride
> For one hour's perfect bliss, to tread the grass
> Of England once again, and hear and see,
> With such a dear Companion at my side.

They went directly to London, where they stayed in
the Montagus' apartment (Basil and Laura were in
Cambridge) and had the first meeting of the five Wordsworths since their childhood. Richard was a successful
London solicitor; Christopher came up from Cambridge
to be with them; and John, by a happy accident, arrived
from his voyage to India while they were all there. It was
a joyous reunion.

Dorothy and William spent three weeks in London, then took two days to visit the Cooksons, who were at Windsor. Their Uncle William Cookson was then a canon of St. George's Chapel at Windsor. He had apparently long since forgiven William and was happy for him now, for his success as a poet and for his forthcoming marriage to Mary. He was overjoyed to see Dorothy.

This was the uncle Dorothy had gone to live with at Forncett Rectory when she was seventeen, and she had spent many happy years with him and his wife and children. She had been content there, cultivating a little garden and running a small school for neighborhood children. Her brothers had visited her there from time to time, but her joy "above all joys" had been William's rare visits before her uncle forbade them. It had been during William's visit to her on her nineteenth birthday, when they had walked together on the gravel path in the garden, pouring out their thoughts and their hopes to one another, that they had first begun to talk of someday living together in a little cottage of their own.

While living with her uncle, Dorothy had had a taste of a more worldly life, but she knew even then that she would prefer the simplicity of life with William. As Canon of Windsor, Mr. Cookson had been invited to spend some months at Windsor Castle, and in the summer of 1792, while William was in Blois, Dorothy had met the royal family. She went for long drives in a beautiful carriage, saw horse races, and went to balls, but she remained shy and unassuming, never acquiring the elegant manners of high society. While she was there, she felt herself in a dream world:

I reached Windsor on the 9th of August and I was charmed with it. When I first set foot upon the terrace I could scarcely persuade myself of the reality of the scene. I fancied myself treading upon fairy ground, and that the country around was brought there by enchantment.

Now, after an enjoyable visit with the Cooksons, William and Dorothy said good-bye to their brothers in London and left for Gallow Hill, arriving there on September 24. Sara and Joanna Hutchinson came soon after, and then Jack and George Hutchinson arrived. Tom, of course, was already there with Mary.

Ten days later, on October 4, 1802, Mary Hutchinson was married to William Wordsworth at nearby Brompton Church. It was a difficult day for Dorothy. Too overwrought to attend the ceremony, she remained at home in an upstairs bedroom until Sara, who had also remained home to prepare the wedding breakfast, came to tell her they were returning from church. Dorothy ran from the house and threw herself on William. He and Jack led her to the house, "and there I stayed to welcome my dear Mary." Had they, in their concern for Dorothy, forgotten Mary at the church?

After the wedding breakfast William, Mary, and Dorothy headed back to Grasmere, a strange trio indeed. They traveled the road Dorothy and William had walked with such eager anticipation just three years before. And so began Dorothy's brave and quiet surrender of her joy at William's marriage.

Chapter 21

My Heart's Best Treasure Was No More

Mary became a devoted wife and sister, and she and William shared a happy marriage for almost fifty years. Her serenity and selflessness became the rock on which the entire Wordsworth family depended.

William continued to write poetry for many years after his marriage, and he was ultimately named Poet Laureate of England. But he was never again able to match that surge of creative power by which he had been inspired in the spring of 1802.

Before his marriage William had been totally devoted to poetry. He probably had misgivings about whether he could become responsible for a wife, and ultimately for children, and still remain dedicated to his high calling as a poet. That his poetry declined after his marriage is answer enough that he could not.

Cared for by a devoted wife and sister (Coleridge said that Mary and Dorothy anticipated William's every wish, that they all but ate and drank for him) and assured finally of financial security, William found himself becoming part of the Establishment. As he became the father of a large family—Mary bore him three sons and two daughters—and a good citizen of the community, he became increasingly conservative in his politics and orthodox in his religion. In fact, he soon returned to the Church of England, in which he had been brought up. The tragic death of his brother John in 1805, and then the death in 1812 of two of his children, within six months of each other, no doubt precipitated this.

A lessening of the time spent with Coleridge was certainly another contributing factor in the decline of William's poetry. Once there were small children in the cottage, there was no longer room for visitors, nor were the Wordsworths happy to have Coleridge drop in late at night, as had been his custom, and then sit up talking until the early hours of the morning. And so the communication between the two poets began to lessen.

Then in 1810 a misunderstanding caused a final break in the friendship of these two who had been so mutually inspiring to one another. William made a casual remark about Coleridge's addiction to opium, and Basil Montagu thoughtlessly repeated it to Coleridge, who was so hurt that he broke off the relationship immediately. Coleridge, who years before had said of William, "I speak with heart-felt sincerity and (I think) unblinded judgement, when I tell you that I feel myself a little man by his side," was heartbroken. And with the ending of the friendship came the final withering of Coleridge's poetic ability. He needed William to inspire him and to spur him on, and his powers declined rapidly after the break.

But William's decline was almost more dramatic than

Coleridge's. While William was undeniably the greater partner, he too needed Coleridge's encouragement. When they parted William was crippled also. Some years later a reconciliation was effected, but the relationship never resumed its original intensity.

And so the years after William's marriage can be described as relatively unexciting.

By 1808 the house at Town End had become much too small for the Wordsworths. They were "crammed into our little nest, edge-full," Dorothy wrote. For there were now three children—John, Dora, and Thomas—and Mary was expecting a fourth. Sara Hutchinson was living with them, and they had a nurse for the children. Friends were constantly visiting. The children's noise was heard in every corner of the house. William had no study of his own, but worked in a crowded sitting room, the children often playing at his feet.

In May of that year they decided to move to nearby Allan Bank, where they would have more space and more privacy. But once there, they discovered a different problem. The chimneys smoked. No sooner were the dishes washed and put away at the conclusion of a meal than they were covered with smoke and unfit to be used at the next meal. Furniture, carpets, newly sewn curtains quickly became dirty, and often, on a windy day, the house was so full of smoke that everyone had to go to bed, their eyes stinging. They withstood this discomfort until June 1811, when they moved into the old Grasmere vicarage, a smaller but more manageable home than Allan Bank.

But it was here that tragedy struck. In June of the following year four-year-old Catherine died suddenly of a "seizure." Six months later sweet-tempered, thoughtful, book-loving little Thomas, his father's favorite and the one whom William thought of as "the future companion of his studies," died also, of pneumonia following measles. The family was distraught.

Some of William's sorrow can be felt in the sonnet he wrote after Catherine's death:

> Surprised by Joy—impatient as the Wind
> I turned to share the transport—Oh! with whom
> But Thee, deep buried in the silent tomb,
>
> . . .
> . . . when I stood forlorn,
> Knowing my heart's best treasure was no more;
> That neither present time, nor years unborn
> Could to my sight that heavenly face restore.

The following year, unable any longer to bear the sight of the churchyard where the two children were buried, and which the vicarage overlooked, the Wordsworths moved to Rydal Mount, a lovely old house on a hill two miles from Grasmere, along the Ambleside Road. Here they remained for the rest of their lives.

About the same time William was appointed distributor of stamps for Westmorland and part of Cumberland, including Penrith. His job entailed collecting Inland Revenue duties for all legal documents, wills, licenses, pamphlets, books, papers, and insurance policies. The position carried with it great responsibility and much work. While the pay was not large, it did provide a steady income and made it possible for the Wordsworths to live comfortably. The post was, in fact, suitable for the son of a country lawyer.

William and Mary were now able to employ an adequate staff of servants at Rydal Mount, but they continued to live frugally. They practiced strict economy in their daily living, but William was finally able to indulge his passion for traveling. The house remained, however, another example of his belief in "plain living, high thinking, no pretense."

William's health remained good throughout his life. He was always an active countryman, and he continued to walk in all kinds of weather as tirelessly as when he had been young. When he was sixty, Dorothy wrote, "He is still the crack skater on Rydal Lake, and as to climbing of mountains, the hardiest and youngest are yet hardly a match for him."

In his seventies he was described as a big man (he was about five feet, ten inches) but slightly stooped, with a prominent brow and nose. His eyes remained deep and luminous. Ralph Waldo Emerson called his face "weather-beaten and corrugated, especially the large nose." This, no doubt, was the result of his years of walking out-of-doors. Physically and mentally, he was a vigorous man. He ran, he skated, he walked for hours. And he continued to work outdoors. When he was seventy-four, Mary casually mentioned that he was "too tired by hard work in the Hay-field" to write.

He wandered for exercise, but he also wandered to see the world around him. And he never completely lost the eye that made him see more than most men see.

His son-in-law, Edward Quillinan, his daughter Dora's husband, affectionately called him "wandering Willie." He called himself "the wandering poet of Winandermere". But he never lost his delight in the Lake District and in his own backyard. He knew every tree, every moss-covered rock, and the effects of light and shadow made by the sunlight. He might have been a professional landscape gardener, and indeed, he encouraged one of his grandsons to do this. In this respect, he was well ahead of his time.

William also liked to drop in casually on his neighbors, and enjoyed playing a rubber of whist with them and with his many friends in the evening. He attended breakfasts and dinners in London and occasionally went to the theater and the opera there. He and Mary gave large dinners at their home also, and had picnics on the island in Lake Windermere or informal gatherings in their own hayfield. Mary was a gracious hostess and entertained a constant stream of houseguests.

William maintained his love of children throughout his life. He was often seen "in the middle of a hedge, cutting switches for half-a-dozen children, who were pulling at his cloak or gathering about his heels."

He expressed interest in the "poetesses of Great Britain." It was his contention that no one took notice of women writers, and he seriously considered writing an article on the subject. He never did, though, partly because he decided that there would be little public interest in the subject.

He was delighted with his own little cousin, Emmeline Fisher, granddaughter of his Uncle William Cookson, who was writing verses at the age of eight. He encouraged her, but worried lest she not be brought up as a normal young girl.

Mary, for her part, cared for her grandchildren (they often stayed with her), nursed the sick in the area, and quietly mothered Coleridge's son Hartley, who lived in Ambleside and often walked with William. While Mary appeared meek and quiet, she was a great source of strength to William, who loved and respected her and relied on her judgment.

He derived much pleasure from the fact that she had composed two lines in his poem about daffodils, "I Wandered Lonely As a Cloud":

> They flash upon that inward eye
> Which is the bliss of solitude.

He often referred to them as "the two best lines in it." She was content and happy as his wife.

Through the years William never changed his habit of composing out-of-doors. Once, when a stranger asked the maid to show him to the poet's study, she took him to the library and said, "This is the master's *library*, but he *studies* in the fields." Physical exercise, love of nature, landscape gardening, being with people, reading, and the joy of his own poetry—these remained his pleasures throughout life.

He maintained his interest in the things he had always loved, but there was sadness. His friends Coleridge and Lamb both died in 1834, and his school friend John

Fleming, in 1835. In June 1835 Sara Hutchinson, who had made her home with the Wordsworths for the last thirty years and who had occupied a very special place in the hearts of all who knew her, died quickly and unexpectedly of rheumatic fever.

Perhaps the greatest blow to William, though, was the tragedy of Dorothy. She had been ill several times and in severe pain over the last few years, but each time she had recovered. Not so now. During Sara's last illness, Dorothy also appeared to be dying. She soon recovered physically, although she was never again able to walk, but her mind, that "mansion for all lovely forms," was shattered. She had what today would be diagnosed as arteriosclerosis (hardening of the arteries) of the brain, and lived in a strange half-world for the remaining twenty years of her life. William cared for her tenderly and faithfully, his only consolation being that her memory for poetry remained unimpaired.

In 1839, when he was sixty-nine years old, William received an honorary law degree from Oxford University. When he rose to accept it, he received a tremendous ovation from the undergraduates. This tribute from the "young enthusiasts," whom he had always loved and believed in, was extremely gratifying to him and echoed in his memory for many years after.

On March 31, 1843, he received an offer from the Lord Chamberlain, Earl de la Warr, to become Poet Laureate of England. His friend Robert Southey had held the post until his death ten days before. "Poet Laureate" is an honor accorded an eminent British poet by the reigning monarch. It names him chief poet of the kingdom for the remainder of his life. This honor, awarded for excellence, carries with it the duty of composing verses for court occasions and significant national events. At the time William was seventy-three years old, and he declined the honor, saying he was too old and might have difficulty writing commemorative poems. Sir Robert Peel, then Prime Minister, guaranteed that nothing would be required of him, and he accepted.

He was asked only once to write a poem for a public occasion. This occurred four years later when Albert, Prince Consort of Queen Victoria, was elected Chancellor of Cambridge University. At this time William's beloved daughter Dora, who had in many ways taken Dorothy's place at her father's side, was dying, and writing was extremely difficult for him. With the help of Dora's husband, Edward Quillinan, however, he did write an ode, which was then set to music. It was the last poem William was to write.

Three years later, in March 1850, William caught cold and then developed pleurisy. He recovered from this, but never again regained his strength. On April 23, just after his eightieth birthday, as he lay in bed listening to the sounds of a newborn spring drifting in through the windows—sounds that he had loved so much—he quietly passed away.

And so, over the years, William had gone from a fiery young radical, ready to reform the world, to a middle-aged moderate, caught up with the cares and responsibilities of his family. And so he continued until his death.

The rebellious passion of the young boy had given way to the conservative control of the older man. The wandering poet of Winandermere had come home. But he had lost "the visionary gleam." "The glory and the dream" had all but disappeared.

Bibliography

Babenroth, A. C., *English Childhood*. New York: Columbia
    University Press, 1922.
Beatty, Frederika, *William Wordsworth of Dove Cottage*.
    New York: Bookman Associates, 1964.
————, *William Wordsworth of Rydal Mount*. New York:
    Dutton, 1939.
Blanchard, Frances, *Portraits of Wordsworth*. London: George
    Allen & Unwin, 1959.
Burton, Elizabeth, *The Pageant of Georgian England*. New
    York: Charles Scribner's Sons, 1967.
Clark, Colette, ed., *Home at Grasmere*. Bristol, England:
    Pelican Books, 1960.
De Selincourt, Ernest, ed., *Letters of William and Dorothy
    Wordsworth: The Early Years 1787–1805*, rev. by Ches-
    ter L. Shaver. London: Oxford University Press, 1967.
Halliday, F. E., *Wordsworth and His World*. New York:
    Viking Press, 1970.
Hill, Douglas, *Georgian London*. London: Macdonald & Com-
    pany, 1970.
Hirsh, Diana, *The World of Turner (1775–1851.)* New York:
    Time-Life Books, 1969.
Knight, William, ed., *Letters of the Wordsworth Family from
    1787 to 1855*. Vol. I. New York: Haskell House Pub-
    lishers, 1969.
Legouis, Emile, *The Early Life of William Wordsworth, 1770–
    1798: A Study of the Prelude*, 2nd ed.; trans. by T. W.
    Matthews. New York: Russell and Russell, 1965.

———, ed., *William Wordsworth and Annette Vallon*, rev. ed. Hamden, Conn.: Shoe String Press, 1967.

Lewis, Wilmarth S., *Three Tours Through London in the Years 1748, 1776, 1797*. New Haven: Yale University Press, 1941.

Maclean, C. M., *Dorothy and William Wordsworth*. New York: Octagon Books, 1972.

Margoliouth, H. M., *Wordsworth and Coleridge, 1795–1834*. Hamden, Conn.: Archon Books, 1966.

Moorman, Mary, *William Wordsworth, The Early Years*. London: Oxford University Press, 1968.

Nesbitt, George L., *Wordsworth*. New York: Pegasus, 1970.

Noyes, Russell, *William Wordsworth*. New York: Twayne Publishing Company, 1971.

———, *Wordsworth and the Art of Landscape*. Bloomington: Indiana University Press, 1968.

Purkis, John, *A Preface to Wordsworth*. New York: Charles Scribner's Sons, 1970.

Rawnsley, Eleanor F., *Grasmere in Wordsworth's Time* (pamphlet). Kendal, England: Titus Wilson, n.d.

Read, Herbert, *Wordsworth*. London: Faber and Faber, 1965.

Reed, Henry, ed., *Memoirs of William Wordsworth Poet-Laureate*. Vol. I. By Christopher Wordsworth. New York: AMS Press, 1966.

Reeve, F. A., *Cambridge*. New York: Hastings House, 1964.

Richardson, Albert E., *Georgian England (1700–1820)*. London: B. T. Batsford, 1931.

Schneider, Ben Ross, Jr., *Wordsworth's Cambridge Education*. Cambridge, England: Cambridge University Press, 1957.

Sperry, Willard L., *Wordsworth's Anti-Climax*. Cambridge, Mass.: Harvard University Press, 1935.

Thompson, T. W., *Wordsworth's Hawkshead*. London: Oxford University Press, 1970.

Trevelyan, G. M., *Illustrated History of England*. London: Longmans, 1962.

Bibliography

Wordsworth, William, *The Prelude*. Edited by Ernest De Selincourt. London: Oxford University Press, 1969.

————, *Selected Poetry*. Introduction by Mark Van Doren. New York: Random House, 1950.

Wordsworth Poetry and Prose. With essays by Samuel Taylor Coleridge, William Hazlitt, and Thomas De Quincey, and introduction by David Nichol Smith. Oxford: The Clarendon Press, 1960.

Wordsworth's Guide to the Lakes. Introduction by Ernest De Selincourt. London: London: Oxford University Press, 1970.

Index

Index of Poems Mentioned

(asterisks [*] indicate poems quoted partially or in full)